HAM ... RY

Stephen Mc... ...ook is geared to helping new Christians find their feet as they begin to grow in their new-found faith. It is straight-forward, honest and realistic as it works out what it means to know and follow Jesus Christ. Rich in practical help and thoroughly grounded in Scripture this book can help 'old hands' get refocused as well as providing building blocks for the new Christian. It will prove to be an enormously helpful resource for those running nurture groups.

Andy Bathgate

A NEW KIND OF LIVING

OF LIVING

Stephen McQuoid

Christian Focus

HAMILTON COLLEGE LIBRARY

© Stephen McQuoid
ISBN 1 85792 396 0
Published in 1998
by
Christian Focus Publications,
Geanies House, Fearn, Ross-shire,
IV20 1TW, Great Britain.

Contents

ACKNOWLEDGEMENT

I would like to thank my father and my
brother Jeremy, as well as Jim Brown, for
their careful reading of this book.
All of their comments proved useful.

A special thanks to my wife Debbie for
all of her encouragement and support.

Chapter 1

The Great Decision

Making decisions is part of everyday life. Some decisions are about trivial matters; others are big, and may lead to great changes in our lives.

The most important decision I have ever made was in choosing to commit my life to Jesus Christ and become a Christian. I handed over the control of my life to him in the belief that he could forgive my past and make use of my future. This decision has made a bigger difference in my life than any other; indeed, my life has been completely revolutionised as a result.

A person may not feel any different when he becomes a Christian, but that does not alter the fact that a number of important things happen to us the moment we trust in Christ. Let me explain some of them.

Forgiven

As soon as a person accepts Jesus Christ as Saviour and Lord, he is forgiven. The past, whatever it contains, is buried and a brand new life has begun. We have all done things that we regret – mistakes we have made, people we have hurt, situations where we deliberately did the wrong thing. God knows all about this. It is possible to keep secrets from even the closest of friends, but nothing escapes God's attention.

Not only does he see the sins we commit, he can read our very thoughts and knows our motives. Wherever my imagination takes me he is there in all his holiness observing the corruption of my thought processes.

How can a God who is perfect and knows all about my sin still accept me? The answer is simple. Jesus has taken the full punishment for my sin and when I asked him for forgiveness, I was completely forgiven. Jesus himself has cleansed me, removing all my guilt. God, therefore, declares me to be faultless, or righteous. Now, when God observes my life, he does not see all the wrong that I have done, rather he sees Jesus living in me, transforming me into the kind of person he wants me to be.

God the Father

This cleansing from sin makes me fit for God's presence. No longer is there a barrier separating me from him. I have access into his presence and I can enjoy this great privilege without fear. But that is not the end of the matter. God actually makes me his son. In John 1:12 we read, *Yet to all who receive him, to those who believe in his name, he gives the right to become children of God.* God has a family comprised of every true Christian and the decision to surrender to the Lordship of Jesus Christ automatically gives us the right to call God 'Father'. The Christian life is about a relationship with God that develops and comes into maturity. As this new life begins, God is not some distant autocrat, he is not remote, for we begin our relationship with him as his child.

Sometimes people struggle with the idea of God as a Father. This may be because experiences within their own families have scarred them. For some the word 'father' carries very negative connotations. I know people who have no idea who their father is because he walked out on them when they were infants. Others have had fathers who were unloving, even cruel; fathers who neglected them and showed them no respect or were cold and remote. For them the very idea of God being their Father fills them with horror.

But imagine a father who is perfect: a father who wants the very best for his children, one with no weaknesses or failings, who is always consistent and fair in the way he deals with his children. God is such a father.

The Bible has much to say about the character of God. We are told that God is Love. It is not just that he is capable of loving, but by definition he is love. Within human relationships it is entirely possible for our emotions to fluctuate. In a marriage, for example, two people may love each other and make a commitment to one another. However, they find as the years pass, that their love burns less brightly and eventually the feelings they once had for each other are all but gone. The divorce rate in this country testifies to the frailty of human love.

When the Bible tells us that God is love, it refers to a love much greater than human emotion. God's love for us doesn't wane with the passing of time, neither does it require fuel to make it burn more brightly. Indeed it was while we were sinful and rebellious that God demonstrated his love to us in giving us Jesus. This is the kind of love we receive from our Father God.

As God is a loving Father, it follows that he is interested in our lives. All we do and say is observed with watchful eyes. This is a solemn thought, but also a wonderful truth. I remember a number of years ago when I worked as a nurse on a care for the elderly ward, a rather grubby old man was admitted. He was a farmer who had spent all his life working and living in the same isolated spot. It was obvious that he knew little about personal hygiene, his clothes were so engrained with dirt that we immediately threw them out. After a good bath we tried to orientate him to the ward and introduce him to other patients. As the days went on I became very frustrated by some of his unpleasant personal habits. He became the centre of conversation on the ward as well as the brunt of many a joke. Try as we may it was seemingly impossible to persuade him to change his ways. He seemed oblivious to the angry glares and disdaining voices all around.

On one particularly bad day, I angrily said to him, 'Why can't you look after yourself? Do you not care what you look like?' He looked at me and I noticed his eyes were filling with tears. 'Why should I care about myself?' He replied, 'no one else does.' What he said was so true and I began to feel a little of his hurt. His was the pain of loneliness. He had no one who really cared.

For the Christian this will never be the case. God is always interested. He sees our tears and shares in our hurts as well as observing our achievements. Whatever we are doing and wherever we are, he is interested and wants to participate in every aspect of our lives.

A loving father wants what is best for his child. When a father disciplines his child, it is for the child's good; the father gets no pleasure from inflicting pain, but sometimes pain is necessary to make the child a better person.

There will be times when God allows Christians to go through difficult and unpleasant circumstances. It is not that God has ceased to love them. He has not abandoned his children, nor does he want them to suffer unnecessarily. We are, however, being moulded into the kind of people God wants us to be. Many lessons can only truly be learned by hardship.

God will sometimes allow difficult circumstances to come your way so that you learn to depend more on him and less on yourself. Hindsight will often show that difficult times are for our ultimate benefit even though unpleasant. Don't assume that now you are a Christian everything will go smoothly in your life. It won't! But God loves you as his child, and he will never act for any other motive than your best interests.

Eternal Life

Another significant thing that happens to a person who becomes a Christian is that he receives eternal life. The promise of eternal life is not just something that applies to the future, it is true of the present. In 1 John. 5:12-13 we read: *He who has the Son has life ... I write these things to you who believe in the name of the Son of God so that you may know that you have eternal life.* Clearly eternal life is something that begins the moment a person becomes a Christian and never ends.

Like all of mankind we will die physically, but for the Christian this will be a release into a better life in heaven where death will no longer be a threat. In heaven we will not just exist for an endless succession of days, but will enjoy a life far superior to anything that we could have here on earth. Mere duration of time is not in itself meaningful. I am not sure if I would like to continue my present existence forever. But heaven is a paradise where there will be no tears (Rev. 21:4). In heaven there will be no need for wheelchairs or crutches, no glasses or hearing aids, there will be no arthritis, no deformity, no scars and no hurts. These evils and the sin which caused them will have no place in heaven, for it will be a place of absolute joy, prepared for us by Jesus himself.

Heaven is, of course, something we will enjoy in the future. But once understood, it gives us an entirely different perspective of our present life. We don't need to battle our way desperately through the rat race of life trying to build a decent future. The future we already have is the best there is. This future is guaranteed, for it is based on a life giving relationship with Jesus Christ. Heaven will be a continuation of this relationship, but free from the constraints of our mortal bodies.

The Christian life, however, is not just about receiving good things from God. There is an element of responsibility also. There are certain things that God demands of us as his children.

Loving God

First and foremost we muse learn to love God more than anything else. Jesus once told an audience that the greatest commandment was to love God with heart, soul and mind (Matt. 22:37). He also stated that unless someone *hates his father and mother, his wife and children, his brothers and sisters – yes even his own life* (Luke 14:26) then he cannot be a disciple. Of course, Jesus did not mean this literally. He of all people taught us the importance of loving others. However, our love for him must be of such quality that no rivals could exist. He must come first! He must be the single most important person in our lives, and his wishes should be paramount.

A few years ago I was talking to a young Christian about his faith. I had been concerned about him because, as far as I could see, he was not growing very much in his new Christian life. As we talked, the reason for his problem became clear. He was involved in a relationship with a girl who was not a

Christian. She was discouraging him from being too committed to his faith and was certainly dampening his enthusiasm for church activity and reading his Bible.

As we talked he admitted that she was coming between him and his relationship with God. 'I do love God,' he said to me, 'but I love my girlfriend just as much.' That was exactly the problem. This girl meant as much to him as God did, and the resulting conflict made it impossible for him to be properly committed to either relationship. I had to explain to him that if he really wanted to live the Christian life, then his relationship with God must come first, for God will not accept second place in our lives. We need to be single minded in our devotion to him and never allow anything else to threaten his rule in our lives. This kind of devotion is not easy, but it is a prerequisite to a genuine Christian commitment.

Loving Christians

A second responsibility God puts on us as Christians is that we are to love other Christians. In John 13:35 Jesus said, *By this all men will know you are my disciples, if you love one another.* Jesus' followers were a very diverse bunch. Some were poor fishermen, one a tax inspector, another was a doctor and to complete the group there was even a terrorist. It may well have been that these different personalities had their clashes and differences. Some of them might even have been hard to get on with.

But Jesus still told them that they must love each other. After all they were brothers and sisters, members of God's family. Every family has arguments and quarrels, but if the relationships within a family are what they should be, there will also be mutual love and respect.

In much the same way, as soon as you become a Christian you inherit a large family comprised of every true Christian. Someone has said, 'You can choose your friends but not your family'. That certainly is true of the Christian family. Like it or not you are there for other Christians and they are there for you. The church (as we will discover in a later chapter) is your family and you have a duty to love and care for each member.

Deny Self

Thirdly, if we are to live the Christian life then we must be willing to deny ourselves. Jesus said in Matthew 16:24: *If anyone would come after me, he must deny himself and take up his cross and follow me*. Jesus' disciples would have often witnessed the sight of men carrying crosses. This was a sure sign that they were going to their deaths. The cross was a brutal but effective form of execution. It always resulted in the same thing – DEATH.

The implication of what Jesus was saying is stark. If we are to follow him, then we must treat ourselves as though we are dead. A dead person has no rights and no will of his own. In the same way we need to give up all rights, lay aside our self-will and allow

Jesus to take over our lives. He must have absolute rule. Whatever he wants us to do we obey. In every situation we need to make decisions based on what we know of his will. His wishes become our wishes as we surrender unreservedly to his rule in our lives. We need to die to our every whim and desire, so that we can be freed to live only for him.

This may seem an impossibility, but as we grow spiritually, the Holy Spirit will help us daily to live this obedient life. Indeed the Christian life is basically a pathway of obedience. As each day passes, God gives us the strength to serve him, and in so doing draws us into an even closer fellowship with him.

Living our lives for Jesus is the best thing we can do. Whoever surrenders his life to Jesus will enjoy eternal life, but whoever squanders his life by living for himself, will have all eternity to regret his foolishness (Matt. 16:25, 26).

PRAYER:
Father, thank you that I have been forgiven. Thank you that I am able to call you Father and know that you will love me as your child. Thank you also for giving me eternal life, a life that has already begun and will continue even after the death of my body.

Teach me to love you in response to your love, and help me to love and care for my fellow Christians. Help me to deny myself so that I can live my life to please you. Teach me what it means to be obedient to your will. Amen.

Chapter 2

God Within

Having considered some of the benefits and responsibilities of Christianity, it is important to remember that we are not left to live the Christian life alone. We have available to us a powerful helper, the Holy Spirit. Before we think about what the Holy Spirit does, it would be good to think about who he is.

Who is the Holy Spirit?

The first thing we can say about the Holy Spirit is that he is a person and not just a mysterious power. A person could be defined as one who has knowledge, a will and emotions. Jesus referred to the Holy Spirit as *he* (John 14:17) and prayed that the Father would send 'him' as a helper, to be with each Christian. Clearly the Holy Spirit must have knowledge of what we need and how to provide that help. In 1 Corinthians 12:11 we read that the Holy Spirit makes decisions about the 'gifts' he gives to Christians; for this to be possible he must have a will and the ability to make intelligent choices. We also read that the Holy Spirit has emotions. He feels love (Rom. 15:30) and grief (Eph. 4:30).

The fact that the Holy Spirit is a person makes it possible for us to have a relationship with him. It is important to realise this. If he were merely a force we might be asking ourselves 'How can I get more of the Holy Spirit?' Because he is a person we need to ask ourselves 'How can I give myself more fully to this relationship with the Holy Spirit?' The difference will revolutionise our Christian lives.

The second thing we need to realise is that the Holy Spirit is God. He is recognised as the third person in the Trinity, along with the Father and the Son. Peter acknowledged the Holy Spirit's deity when he accused Ananias of lying against God (Acts 5:3-4). The Holy Spirit possesses qualities which are unique to God, namely eternal existence (Heb. 9:14) and omnipresence (Psalm 139:7-10).

The fact that the Holy Spirit is God means that we have as a friend the most powerful person in the universe, a constant companion who will help us to live the kind of lives God requires. Because of his presence in our lives, we don't have to rely merely on our own strength to live the Christian life, but on the power of God.

Now that we have thought about the person of the Holy Spirit, we then want to ask, What does he do? Of the many activities in which the Holy Spirit is engaged, I will mention just four.

Relationship with Christ
Firstly, the Holy Spirit brings us into a living relationship with Jesus Christ. Without his activity, no one could or would become a Christian, for, left to themselves, human beings are spiritually blind and incapable of understanding their spiritual needs.

I have often talked to my non-Christian friends about their sin and God's judgment and yet some of them have never shown any interest. One friend even said to me, 'I know Christianity is the truth, and I can see it works for you, but I just don't think it is for me.' He went on to admit that he was a sinner with no hope of going to Heaven. Remarkably he was not concerned about this. Such blindness is not just intellectual, it is spiritual.

The only cure for spiritual blindness is spiritual revelation. Jesus told his disciples that the Holy Spirit would *convict the world of guilt in regard to sin and righteousness and judgment* (John 16:8). Only when the Holy Spirit does this can a person respond to Christ's love.

Once a person realises his need for forgiveness and commits himself to a relationship with Jesus Christ, the Holy Spirit then gives him a new spiritual life. That person is now *born again*. In John chapter three, Jesus told Nicodemus about his need to be 'born again'. Though a religious leader, Nicodemus had to understand that without this new birth he would never see God's kingdom (John 3:3). Jesus then went on to explain the source of this new life – *No one can enter God's kingdom unless he is born of water and the Spirit* (John 3:5). It is the Holy Spirit who gives us this new life.

A Teacher
Secondly, the Holy Spirit is a teacher. God wants us to know the truth about himself, and the kind of lives

he expects us to live. All of this is revealed by the Holy Spirit. How can we learn about these truths? Our principal source is the 'Word of God', the Bible.

When Jesus was preparing the disciples for his departure, he told them that the Holy Spirit would *teach you all things and remind you of everything I have said to you* (John 14:26). These men were responsible for recording the life and teachings of Christ and the Holy Spirit would ensure that the record was truthful and accurate. The whole Bible is the product of the Spirit's work. Although it was written by ordinary men, they were 'inspired' or prompted by the Holy Spirit to write (2 Pet. 1:21; 2 Tim. 3:16). We have the authoritative guide to faith and lifestyle available within its pages.

As the Holy Spirit is ultimately the author of the Bible, then it is obvious that we need his help to understand it. As we read the Bible with humility and an open heart, the Holy Spirit will 'speak' to us through it.

I can remember as a young teenager going along to a Bible class in my church. We were strongly encouraged to memorise passages of scripture and even given delicious incentives to help us along the way. Though I memorised whole chapters of the Bible, the significance of the passages never really hit home. The problem was essentially a spiritual one. God was a distant stranger and so I could not understand the muffled sounds of his voice. Now that my relationship with God is different, the passages that I have committed to memory have taken on a meaning. I now know that they are a personal message to me from God, and as I think about them, the Holy Spirit enables me to understand what God is saying.

The Holy Spirit, through our study of the Bible, teaches us about God, the truths of our faith and Christian living.

Christlike Character

A third function of the Holy Spirit is to make us Christ-like. Let me tell you about two important Biblical words, *sanctification* and *justification*. When I became a Christian, although I had sinned, God forgave me. But I am more than just forgiven; God treats me as if I have never sinned. I am *not guilty* as far as he is concerned (Rom. 5:1). This is known as justification. It is as if I was on trial in a court room with God as my judge. The judge sees that Jesus has paid the price for my sin and so finds in my favour by acquitting me. It is not that I am morally perfect through becoming a Christian, but God regards me as being not guilty because of what Jesus has done (Rom. 3:24).

At this point sanctification begins. Sanctification is an ongoing process whereby the Holy Spirit makes my relationship with God all the more meaningful. This preparation requires obedience on my part, but also involves the activity of the Holy Spirit in my life (Rom. 15:16). As I surrender my life to God on a daily basis and determine to obey his will, the Holy Spirit moulds me into the kind of person God wants me to be.

IAMILTON COLLEGE LIBRARY

This is obviously not an overnight change; it takes place over many years. I know people who have been Christians for over fifty years and they would be the first to admit that their Christian lives are not what they should be. But the Holy Spirit is at work in their lives to the extent that they and others have noticed a change in their behaviour and attitudes.

Paul gives a description of the kind of person God wants us to be: *But the fruit of the Spirit is love, joy, peace, patience, kindness, goodness, faithfulness, gentleness and self control* (Gal. 5:22, 23). As the Holy Spirit works in us these characteristics will begin to emerge.

Love
Love is the first on the list. Paul tells us that this is the greatest of the Christian virtues (1 Cor. 13:13). God's love toward us was unmerited (Rom. 5:8) and he wants us to learn to love others in the same way. This love is not just a sentimental feeling, it is not the same as liking someone because they are an attractive person. Rather, God wants us to so love others that we will want the best for them and actively seek their highest good, irrespective of who they are.

Joy
Joy is the second characteristic. This is not the same as happiness for the latter depends on our circumstances. As soon as favourable circumstances are removed, happiness quickly disappears. Joy is something we can possess in spite of our

circumstances. Joy is based on our knowledge and appreciation of God and what he has done for us in Christ. Throughout the centuries Christians have suffered all kinds of difficulties, trials, illnesses, persecutions and griefs, and yet have been filled with joy because of their relationship with Jesus Christ.

I think of a Christian friend who suffers from a serious crippling disease, as a result of which she is very restricted in her movements and relies on the help of others to do even the simplest of tasks. In such circumstances it is difficult to imagine how anyone could have a positive outlook on life, yet she is full of joy and an inspiration to all who know her. This joy comes from a delight in God that can accept the most testing of circumstances.

Peace
In a world where fighting, disagreement and disharmony are commonplace, it is a great privilege to experience peace. We have peace with God because of the work of the cross (Rom. 5:1) and this should have an effect on all our relationships. We are to actively promote peace and harmony in our dealings with others (Heb. 12:14) and exert a calming influence wherever there is tension.

Patience
In spite of the number of times we fail God, he is patient with us and does not reject us. This should motivate us to be patient with others, even though they may disappoint or annoy. Patience does not

mean turning a blind eye to the faults of others, but it does mean that we are willing to give someone a second chance, even if common sense tells us not to.

Kindness
Kindness too is something God continually shows us. God has the right to insist on our absolute obedience and to punish us severely if we fail. However he chooses to treat us kindly as a father would treat a child. In response we should show kindness to others around us even though we feel they do not deserve it. The kind person will return a harsh word with a gentle one and be prepared to go the extra mile to help another.

Faithfulness
Faithfulness is a very rare characteristic. It involves reliability, trustworthiness, and dependability. People around us ought to be able to share confidences with us knowing that we will not let them down. It should be obvious to all that we can be trusted with any task and that we will be consistent in carrying out any duty. The faithful person is a true friend who can be relied on with confidence.

Gentleness
Gentleness is often equated with weakness, but nothing can be farther from the truth. Christ was gentle but had the strength of character to take on the establishment. Gentleness is strength under control. The gentle person is the one who can act

appropriately in every circumstance. When he should be angry (when confronted by sin, injustice, oppression) then he is, but he is never angry at the wrong time.

Self-control
This is the characteristic which gives us victory over our selfish desires. It is self-control that prevents us from indulging in sexual immorality or lust. It keeps us from greed or selfishness. Self-control means that we can live in this corrupt world without succumbing to its temptation.

Humanly speaking, displaying these characteristics in our lives may seem an impossibility. In fact it is! But it is the Holy Spirit's function to produce all these Christlike graces in us, and he will do it, little by little, if we allow him.

Being Filled

It is important to note, however, that we need to be 'filled' with the Holy Spirit if this transformation is to take place. Every Christian is 'indwelt' with the Holy Spirit, indeed it is impossible for a person to be a Christian without the Holy Spirit living in him (Rom. 8:9). Being 'filled' with the Spirit, however, is a different matter.

Suppose I invited you to stay at my home but, when you arrived, I allowed you no further than the hall way! Strictly speaking, you would be living in my house, but having no access to it. The bedrooms and bathroom upstairs would be out of bounds, as would the living room, dining room and kitchen. You would be a resident, but one with no liberty.

This is how some Christians treat the Holy Spirit. He indwells them but they do not give him access to every aspect of their lives for fear he might change more of their lives than they want him to. If we are to become like Christ, it is essential that the Holy Spirit is not hindered in any way, but has complete access to, and freedom to influence our lives.

How then can we be filled with the Holy Spirit? The first thing we must do is to make a deliberate decision that Christ is to be Lord of our lives as well as Saviour. That will involve surrendering ourselves to him so that his wishes become our wishes. In effect, we are relinquishing our own rights and desires so that we can be more available to him.

Secondly we must study the Bible in order to learn how God wants us to live. Bible study should never be just an academic exercise, rather it should be seen as a blueprint for our lives. As we study, we need to obey what we have learned, putting it into practice in our daily lives.

Thirdly we need to keep in fresh daily fellowship with God. This will involve reading the Bible and talking to God in prayer. As we share our lives with him in this way, our relationship with him grows and matures. It is in this way that the Holy Spirit fills our lives and transforms us.

As the Holy Spirit fills us, we find a new power in our lives. It is this power that the Holy Spirit utilises as he directs us into service for God. This is his fourth function. In Acts 13:2-4 the Holy Spirit commanded the church in Antioch to send Paul and Barnabas on a specific task. Not only did the Holy Spirit give the command but he also accompanied them all the way, empowering them to fulfil their task.

Not everyone is called to serve God in the same way, but every Christian is called to serve. We all have a task to perform. Not only will the Holy Spirit burden us to serve God, but he will also equip us to fulfil whatever task we are called to do (we will think about this equipment in a later chapter). We must ensure that we are sensitive to his voice and obedient to his every command.

PRAYER:
Father, Thank you for the Holy Spirit who lives in me, making it possible for me to have a relationship with you and your Son, Jesus Christ. Thank you that I will never be alone because the Holy Spirit is my constant companion.

Help me to be teachable and allow the Holy Spirit to so fill my life, that I become like Jesus. Instil in me love, joy and peace, help me to be patient, kind, faithful and gentle as well as self-controlled. I want to reflect the life of Jesus and I know that requires a filling of the Holy Spirit.

Fill me so that I can live a life that pleases you. Amen.

Chapter 3

'Let's Start Talking'

Relationships are an important element in all of our lives. One thing I have discovered over the years is that all relationships need to be worked at. It is impossible for two people to remain close friends if there is little contact between them.

When it comes to the spiritual realm, things are no different. Although God lives in me through his Holy Spirit, and will never leave me, I still need to work at my relationship with him. This will involve communication on a regular basis which is where prayer comes into the equation.

What is Prayer?
To put it simply, prayer is the means by which we can come into direct contact with God. God speaks to us through his word and in other ways, and we can speak to him as we pray. It is important to note, however, that prayer is more that just two friends chatting casually together. I have many friends with whom I like to converse and when I am with one of them, we talk as equals. I hope that all of my friendships are mutually rewarding, but I am not dependant on my friends to any great extent. When it comes to my relationship with God the situation is altogether different. We do not relate to each other

as equals, for God is infinitely greater and more powerful than I am. I depend on God completely and recognise that without him I would be nothing.

The realisation of God's greatness makes the thought of prayer even more wonderful. At any time, wherever I am, I can approach God, the Creator of the universe, and I can be confident that he is listening. There is no queuing system, I do not have to book in advance, I can enjoy immediate access and know that God is there. I do not even have to say the words out loud for he can read my mind. While driving in my car, waiting for a bus, watching T.V. or just simply relaxing in the privacy of my living room, God is listening and I can talk to him knowing that he will not ignore me.

One thing that amazes me is that God actually wants me to talk to him. Once when I was quite a young Christian, I had a moment of doubt and wondered if God would have the time to listen to my insignificant voice. Surely he is very busy and has many important tasks to attend to. Then it dawned on me just how important it is to my own father when I spent time with him and we talk. God is also my Father, and he enjoys my company. He considers what I have to say to be of value. God takes pleasure when I express my love to him. He wants to share in my decisions and is anxious that I bring my concerns to him. God is not an austere potentate, but a loving Father who enjoys listening to his children.

Clearly, prayer is important to God, but it is also vital for us. Through prayer we can tell God about our needs. We can bring situations to him that we cannot deal with ourselves. God already knows about the difficulties we are facing and is waiting for us to share them with him. Nothing is impossible for God, so these requests can be brought with confidence. One Christian writer has said that prayer is like a missile, it can be fired at any target on earth, travels undetected at the speed of thought, and hits its target every time.

Without God's help we could never successfully live the Christian life. After a few days, relying on our own strength, we would collapse. It is through prayer that we seek and find God's strength, as he answers our request for help.

Perhaps this is why the Bible commands us to *pray continually* (1 Thess. 5:17). Without prayer we are helpless, isolated and weak. Through prayer we can experience the fellowship and strength of God as we share together.

How do I Pray?

If prayer is so important, then how do I pray? What am I supposed to say? On one occasion Jesus was teaching his disciples how they should pray (Matt. 6:9-13). The 'Lord's Prayer', as it is known, was not meant to be a standard set of words that we utter every time we want to talk to God, but it does give us a 'model' of the kind of things we should be thinking about when we pray.

Worship

Jesus began this prayer with the words *Hallowed be your name*. In stating that God's name was to be 'hallowed' (or holy) Jesus was indicating that we are to recognise God's true value and regard him with awe when we pray. God is our Father. We do have an intimate relationship with him, however we cannot be casual as we relate to him. We need to recognise his greatness and approach him with respect. Worship and adoration should therefore be important components in our prayers.

Think of God as Creator, think of his awesome power and creativity. Bear in mind that God is utterly holy, without fault, consistent in all he does. Think also of his great love, compassion and kindness. When you meditate on these qualities it would be impossible not to worship and adore God.

Submission

Next Jesus said, *Your kingdom come, your will be done on earth as it is in Heaven*. God is already King of the universe and has the right to demand our absolute obedience, but we need to recognise this in our own lives. The most important thing to remember when we pray is not what we want, but what God wants. Prayer is not making demands of God (though we are told to make requests [Phil. 4:6] and we can do this boldly), rather we want God's will to be done in our lives. In this sense, through prayer, we bring ourselves into line with God's will. We can ask God for things, indeed we should ask, but we accept whatever answers God gives. In our requests, there should be the recognition that our ultimate desire is for God's will to be done in our lives.

Requests

Jesus then listed three requests, one for physical needs and two for spiritual. *Give us this day our daily bread* was the first. There is nothing wrong with asking God for material benefits, provided our motive is not greed and we are willing to put all we possess at God's disposal.

I remember when my wife and I got married we did not have a suitable place to live. On many occasions we prayed asking God to provide us with a house. We were not being greedy for this was a genuine need. Not only did we pray for a house, but we wanted one within a stone's throw of our church so that it could be available to Christians in the area. God answered those prayers in a miraculous way and confirmed to us that he was interested in our physical needs as well as our spiritual ones.

Confession

The final two requests relate to the need for forgiveness, *forgive us our debts as we also have forgiven our debtors*, and victory over temptation, *lead us not into temptation but deliver us from the evil one*. Firstly we need to consider the issue of forgiveness.

When I became a Christian, every sin I had ever committed was forgiven. I now have eternal life and a relationship with God that cannot be taken from me. Despite all that has happened I still have a sinful nature and though I try not to sin, there are times when I am unable to prevent myself from doing so. When I sin my relationship with God is not broken, but it is affected.

When I was young I was a habitual liar. My family used to get very frustrated with me because half the time they never knew whether or not I was telling the truth. My father in particular did not like it when I lied. He got very annoyed. At no point was my relationship with him under threat, he would always be my father and I would be his son. It was inevitable, however, that my behaviour sometimes made it difficult for us to be friends, and so communication with each other was a little strained as a result.

There have been times in my Christian life when I have found it difficult to pray because God seemed quite remote. Often the problem was my sin. I knew I had done wrong, and I realised that God was concerned. It is difficult to be in the presence of someone who makes me feel uncomfortable. It was not that God had disowned me, he would never do that, but I still feel awkward talking to him knowing that he is aware of my sin.

This is the very reason that Jesus told us to pray for forgiveness, even as Christians. We need to ensure that nothing gets in the way of our relationship with God our Father. We simply need to confess the sins we can remember committing, as well as those we do not remember, and we can be sure they are forgiven (1 John 1:9). This can be done whenever we take the time to pray.

Spiritual Protection

Secondly we need to consider Jesus' words on temptation: *Lead us not into temptation, but deliver us from the evil one*. We live in a real world and would be deceiving ourselves if we thought we were impervious to temptation. Not only do we have our sinful human nature to contend with, but we also have a powerful enemy in the Devil. The Bible sometimes refers to him as 'the Tempter'. Satan is very subtle and can trip us up or cause us to stumble.

It would not be right to ask God to remove us from any danger because he has placed us where we are to be a witness for him. What we should pray for is the strength to resist any temptation that comes our way. As we pray we are tapping into the greatest power of all and we will find the strength to live the kind of lives God wants us to live, if only we ask for it.

This then is an example of how to pray, and some of the things we should be praying about. In our prayers we should worship God, recognising how great God is and the privilege of having immediate access to him. We should make requests for daily needs, bearing in mind that his will is paramount and whatever answer he gives, we will accept it gratefully knowing God has our best interests at heart. Confession of sin should also be an important element in our prayers. Ask God for his continued forgiveness and for the strength to resist any spiritual temptations that Satan might put in our way. Prayer is a vital defence against the Devil as he tempts us to sin.

The above list is, of course, not exhaustive. It is just the beginning. There are many more things you will learn to pray about as you become more comfortable with praying. For example, the Bible talks about intercession, that is praying for, or on behalf of others. Jesus prayed for Peter (Luke 22:31, 32) and Paul told the Christians in Ephesus to pray for each other (Eph. 6:18). I have noticed as I have matured spiritually, that I am spending an increasing amount of time praying for others, and less time praying about my needs. Perhaps this is a good balance to strike.

Does God Answer Prayer?

People have often asked me this question, 'Does God answer prayer?' Jesus assured us that he does (Matt. 6:10). We may not always get exactly what we have been asking for. Remember that the most important thing in prayer is God's will. Often God's answer to our request is 'yes', as in the case of Hannah, when she asked God for a son (1 Sam. 1). Sometimes God says 'no' to a request, for example when Paul asked for his *thorn in the flesh* to be removed (2 Cor. 12:7-10). On other occasions God may ask us to 'wait' before he grants a request. This is what happened to Zechariah and Elizabeth when they prayed for a son (Luke 1:5-13).

Often it is easy to know what answer God is

giving. I once prayed for a particular job. There was a vacancy and I knew I was capable of filling it, but I was also concerned about what God wanted. I prayed about it and later discovered that someone else had got the position. In that case, God very clearly said 'no'. On other occasions I prayed for things and got them, obviously God's answer was 'yes'. But how will we know if God is just telling us to wait?

I really don't have a deeply theological answer to this problem. I do believe, however, that God can speak to us as we pray and if we can learn to be sensitive to this inner voice, he will reveal his will to us and even burden us to pray for particular things. This sensitivity is not something we develop overnight. Like most things in the Christian life, it comes through a slow learning process. As we get to know God better and our relationship with him becomes more intimate, so we will learn how to distinguish his answers to our prayers. As a learner in the art of prayer I can only say how exciting it is to know that God is speaking to me and is able to reveal his will for my life. Be patient. You too will discover this excitement!

Whatever answers we receive, God only wants what is best for us and we must realize that we will not always know what the future holds for us. If God does say no, he will give us the strength and grace to cope with whatever the situation we are in.

On a purely practical note, I have found it very helpful to use a prayer diary. If there is something I feel needs prayer, then I write it down. This not only helps me to remember what to pray for, but also gives me reasons for rejoicing as these prayer requests get answered. Nothing encourages me more when I get down to pray, than to see a page full of prayer requests that have been crossed off the list because they have been answered. The only disadvantage of keeping a prayer diary is that it reminds me of how seldom I praise God for answering my prayer.

PRAYER:
Father, thank you that you are only a prayer away and that I can talk to you at any time. Thank you that you will always listen to me and answer my prayers.

Teach me to pray. Help me to draw close to you so that I can understand your will and experience the joy of your fellowship.

I want our relationship to grow, because you are my Father and I am your child. Please speak to me as I pray. Amen.

Chapter 4

Persistence, Faith and Humility

In the previous chapter we looked at the 'model prayer' that Jesus taught his disciples. Of course that is not to say that we have exhausted the subject. On the contrary we have only just begun. I am still a learner as far as prayer is concerned, and am discovering more about the subject both from what I read in the Bible and through my own experience of praying.

I am also discovering the importance, not just of what Jesus said in the 'Lord's Prayer', but also some of the other lessons he taught his disciples.

Ask, Seek and Knock

On one occasion Jesus was teaching his disciples how to pray. He wanted to emphasize that prayer is very powerful and can accomplish much, provided we really mean what we say. Jesus talked about *asking, seeking and knocking* (Luke 11:9). Not only are we to ask God when we pray, but we should also be seeking for an answer. In other words put ourselves into a position whereby we are able to receive what we are asking for.

Some years ago I asked God to touch the life of a friend of mine so that he would become a Christian. This was one of my first attempts at intercessory prayer. My friend was such a hard person I wondered if God really could break through and bring him to repentance.

One day, completely 'out of the blue', my friend told me he had just become a Christian. I found myself in a state of shock and unprepared to care for this 'baby' Christian. I had been praying for him, but I really didn't believe anything would happen. I wasn't 'seeking'. When God answered my prayer and gave me what I was asking for, it suddenly dawned on me just how empty my prayer had been. On this occasion God answered in spite of my lack of faith. The Bible seems to teach that this is not usually the case.

Not only are we to 'ask' and 'seek', but says Jesus, we should also 'knock'. Our prayers should have a sense of urgency about them. Like a repeated knocking on the door we should persist in asking God, until such time as we get an answer.

Persistence

In order to stress his point about persistent prayer, Jesus told this parable (Luke 11:5-8). A man had a visitor at midnight. The visitor was probably travelling at night so as to avoid the exhausting heat of the day. It was a custom to give hospitality to others, but the host discovered, to his horror, that he had no food in the house.

Rather sheepishly he went to his neighbour's house, knowing full well that his neighbour would be in bed. He knocked on the door, asking for some bread, and was met by the annoyed response 'go away'. Undeterred by this, he continued knocking until his request was answered. No doubt the neighbour who gave him the bread did not do so out of friendship, but simply because the man would not give up.

This according to Jesus is how we should pray. God is not unwilling to answer our prayers, he does not give begrudgingly. He does however want us to be in earnest about our prayers. How can we show that we really mean it? We must pray persistently, and keep going until we get an answer.

I have a friend who asked God for a wife. After several months of praying he could so easily have given up. He believed however that God was not saying 'No' to his request, but just testing his earnestness, and so he continued to pray. Six years later he found the right woman and has been thanking God ever since!

It is this kind of praying that God looks for. People who will not lose heart, but will keep asking.

It would be wrong, however, to assume that God must answer our prayers, simply because we have been at it for a long time. The length of a prayer will not automatically guarantee that we will receive what we have asked for. Jesus said that we don't have the right to a divine hearing simply because of our many words (Mt. 6:7). True prayer is more than just a succession of words, it is about children communicating meaningfully with their Father. If our prayers are to be genuine, then the attitude of our hearts is also important. A correct attitude along with persistence will have its effect. God gages our earnestness and sincerity by the fervency of our prayer life.

Faith

Another of Jesus' parables on prayer gives us a further insight. This time the parable involves a poor widow (Luke 18:1-8). In the ancient world before the advent of our social security programmes, a widow was the most helpless of people. Her husband had been her provider and protector, but now he was dead and she was left to fend for herself.

As Jesus told this story he had in mind all those Christians who have suffered injustice in some way or other. It is only natural for us as Christians to cry to God when we are harmed. We live in a world that is antagonistic towards the Christian faith, to be a follower of Jesus Christ is to go against the crowd and oppose the evils that are engrained in society.

But what happens if we are suffering some injustice, and when we cry to God, there seems no answer; worse still, the situation deteriorates? I know a Christian who worked for a transport company. It was standard practice for the drivers in that company to exaggerate their expenses claims and use company fuel and time for their personal use. This Christian knew that this 'standard practice' was wrong and refused to participate in the crime. At the end of the month when all the expenses claims were submitted, the other drivers realised that they had an honest man in their midst. Suddenly the atmosphere in the work place changed. The Christian found himself under siege with threats and accusations being made against him. He was treated with such hostility by everyone in the firm that he even stopped visiting the company canteen for fear of ridicule.

He cried out to God and asked for help in this difficult situation. No doubt he was hoping that justice would be done. Instead of receiving justice, he got the sack for causing such a disturbance in the company. What should he do in a situation like that? What should we do when we face a similar ordeal? Should we give up and stop praying?

Jesus told the parable of the widow so that his disciples would *always pray and not give up* (v. 1). This widow had suffered an injustice and so went to the Judge. The Judge, upon his own admission, was neither scrupulous nor caring. He had absolutely no reason for answering this woman's call for help. Despite this she pleaded with him and was determined not to give up. She would keep coming before him until she got satisfaction. Eventually the Judge gave in. Not because he wanted to help her, but simply because he wanted a quiet life

In this parable Jesus was contrasting God with the Judge. The contrast could not be greater because God is not only just, he is also loving and is concerned about our lives. The implication is obvious. If a rotten judge like this would grant a poor widow justice, how much more would God grant justice for his own children?

The kind of prayer that God looks for is believing prayer. When we pray we must believe that God is both good and powerful and will answer our prayers appropriately. Indeed there is little point in praying if we do not believe this about God. We need to pray constantly, even when the situation we are in seems impossible to resolve. The very fact that we are continuing to pray is a statement of faith in God. This is the kind of prayer that will be answered.

It is interesting to note Jesus' expression at the end of this parable – *When the Son of Man comes will he find faith on the earth?* (v. 8). Just imagine that I was praying for a situation where an injustice was being committed, and then gave up because of lack of faith. How would I feel if Jesus then came back in power and glory, setting all wrongs to right and dealing with injustice, and was to ask me why I had given up praying? How would I then feel? What answer could I possibly give him? These questions are a great challenge and should inspire Christians to pray, even in the midst of difficult situations, believing that God has the power and the will to make a difference.

Humility

Prayers, however, should not just be persistent and made in faith. We also need to have the right attitude when we pray. Jesus told another parable (Luke 18:9-14) about a Pharisee and a tax collector. In the eyes of Jesus' audience, these two men could not have been more different. Pharisees were well respected religious leaders, while tax collectors were invariably corrupt and despised.

On this occasion the two men were in the temple praying. The Pharisee was on his feet and in his prayer talked about himself with great pride. He thanked God that he was not like ordinary mortals who were dishonest, sinful and unfaithful. More than anything else he was not like that horrible tax collector. Then he proceeded to tell God how good he was with his fasting and his financial support of good causes.

The tax collector, on the other hand, could only think of how unworthy he was in the presence of God. He stood at a distance, hardly even daring to go much past the entrance of the building. In shame he was almost tearing his hair out and was crying to God for mercy. There was no sense of self-righteousness about him. He had many faults which he knew could not be hidden from God, so he openly confessed them and threw himself on God's mercy.

After telling this parable, Jesus went on to explain that the tax collector's prayers would be answered rather those of the Pharisee. Why? Because he approached God with humility. If we think for one moment that we deserve God's love, or that he ought to answer our prayers, that proud attitude will render our prayers powerless. However, when we acknowledge God's generosity towards us and pray realising that we are unworthy of God's love, then we have his ear and can be assured of a response.

Prayer, as we have seen, is communication between us and our Father God. We pray to keep our relationship with him fresh and intimate. Prayer is an act of worship and submission to the will of God, an acknowledgment that God is good and loving and wants the best for us. It is also the means by which we tap into the greatest power in the universe. Our prayer lives, however, must be characterised by persistence, faith and humility.

PRAYER:
Father, thank you for this powerful weapon of prayer. Thank you that you listen to my requests and have the power to change any situation I bring to you.

Help me never to pray empty prayers but to ask, seek and knock. Give me both persistence and faith so that I will never loose heart when I am praying about something. Teach me what it means to be humble so that my attitude in prayer is correct.

Thank you for being a loving Father. Amen.

Chapter 5

The Art of Listening

'Do you own a Bible?' I asked an elderly lady as I stood talking to her on her doorstep. My reason for being in the area was to encourage the people living there to read their Bibles and discover how relevant it is.

A few minutes later she reappeared holding a dust covered bag. 'I found it on top of the wardrobe in the spare room,' she said to me. Opening the bag I found a 1922 copy of the Bible – King James Version of course. Clearly it had not been opened for years, let alone read. It struck me as tragic that such a profound book, the very words of God, could be so neglected by its owner.

To be fair, the old lady did have some excuse; she was not a Christian and so did not feel the need to 'hear' what God had to say to her. Many Christians, however, are also in the habit of ignoring their Bibles. I have spoken to Christians who might spend five minutes twice a week reading the Bible, but that is as far as their interest goes.

What is the Bible?
The Bible is the word of God. It is through this book that God reveals his will for our lives. In the Bible we discover who God is and how we can live lives

that please him. We discover moral values and standards that God wants us to apply in our lives. In the Bible God talks about his love for us and how we can develop and grow as Christians. In short, God has given us the Bible so that we can live the Christian life successfully and come to know him intimately. Why then do so many Christians not give time to reading what God has said?

There could be a number of reasons for this lack. Some people are by nature lazy and so doing anything that involves effort (reading the Bible thoughtfully is demanding) is quite a burden. Others may lead such busy lives that it is difficult to find the time to read. No doubt some people are intimidated by the sheer size of the Bible and are not sure where to start. They spend time thinking about it but they never actually get down to reading the Bible.

Perhaps the main reason why Christians don't spend time reading their Bibles is because they don't believe that God will actually speak to them through what they read. If we believed that God has something important to say to us, and that our lives could be enriched by it, then we would willingly give the time and effort required. I believe that we as Christians need, perhaps more than anything else, to grasp the importance of listening to God's voice as he speaks to us through his word and determine to make this our habit in life.

In the early church, a high priority was given to the apostles' teaching, which would later on be reduced to written form in the Bible (Acts 2:42). Jesus himself had said that we cannot rely on physical food alone if our growth as people is to be healthy, but this must be supplemented by nourishment from God's word (Matt. 4:4). Just as a lack of food would damage our bodies, so depriving ourselves of God's word will stunt our spiritual growth.

Why Read the Bible?

What are the benefits of reading the Bible? The apostle Paul when advising his young friend Timothy told him that *All scripture is God breathed and is useful for teaching, rebuking, correcting and training in righteousness* (2 Tim. 3:16)

First of all the Bible acts as a *teacher*. The Christian faith is based on truths which include both historical events and doctrines. These truths are necessary if we are to have an authentic faith. We need to believe in the truth about God, ourselves, our world, and God's work in our lives. If we were to take away these truths we would have no faith at all for faith cannot exist within a vacuum. There must be something we believe in.

The Bible reveals truth to us. In its pages God reveals himself and allows us a privileged insight into his thoughts and plans. We find truth about ourselves, our human nature and the reason for our existence. The Bible not only tells us about the sin that is destroying humanity, but also about God's remedy through Jesus Christ. We can also discover the truth about the world's future and the hope of heaven that lies before us. All these truths and many more are presented to us in the Bible; they are available if only we are prepared to look.

The Bible also *rebukes* us when our lives are not what they should be. It is a book which deals not only with the truths of our faith, but also with our conduct. How will we be able to make moral decisions in life? What is the basis of our morality? How do we know if the life we are living is wrong? The answers can be found in the Bible. God reveals his standard by which he judges all of our actions, and only by reading the Bible can we assess our lives and see how far short we fall.

Thirdly the Bible *corrects* our false ideas. We live in a world filled with a bewildering mass of ideas, opinions and viewpoints. Some ideas might be correct, or even partly correct, but as Christians we need to be aware that Satan is a great deceiver and loves nothing better than to spread lies and half-truths.

How can we judge whether an idea or belief is truthful? A thing may sound plausible, even attractive, but that does not necessarily make it true. Like the people centuries ago who believed the world was flat, we could be sincere, but at the same time be sincerely wrong! How do we judge the rightness of a belief? The answer is that the Bible tells us. Any false notions or wrong ideas will be corrected as we apply the Bible to our lives. This correcting may be painful; it may destroy some of our pre-conceived ideas and prejudices, but it will save us from the peril of false beliefs.

Finally the Bible *trains us in righteousness*. A

cleansing effect takes place on our minds and lives as we read, and we emerge from Bible study feeling refreshed and renewed. As we immerse ourselves in God's word and obey what it says, the Holy Spirit begins his work in our lives, moulding us, giving us the ability to understand and apply the truth. Gradually we are transformed as the Holy Spirit makes us more like Jesus.

There is of course a reason for this training. Our reading of the Bible is not just an academic exercise. The Holy Spirit trains us through the reading of the Bible, so that we become equipped to do God's work (2 Tim. 3:17). We are able to share this truth with others and the change that takes place in us enables us to live lives which are of service to them.

Some years ago I met a young Christian student who was as unlike my image of what a godly man should be, as could be imagined. Mark was a likeable enough guy, but it was almost impossible to have a serious conversation with him, particularly about Christian matters (perhaps I have a prejudice towards flippant people). He would continually joke about everything and often in an irreverent manner. Mark was loud, discourteous and utterly carefree. Then he began to take his Bible seriously. I don't know what provoked this change of heart, but it became such a serious pursuit that he ended up in Bible college.

It would be wrong of me to claim that Mark experienced a total change of personality. He is still noisy, sometimes rude and continues to have a boyish sense of humour (God wants to refine us as people, not give us a personality replacement). However, it is noticeable how kind and caring Mark has become. He has become a much more self-controlled person and one who wants to be of help to others, both spiritually and practically. In Christian terms, the boy has become a man and is living his life for God's glory, as he serves God as a missionary in Japan.

An Ancient Book

As you begin reading the Bible it is important to realise that it is not just one book but a compilation of sixty six. These books were written over a period of 1,500 years, by people from many different backgrounds and walks of life. Some were kings while others were farmers, nomads and fishermen.

Each writer, though inspired by the Holy Spirit, brought his own character to his writings. The different styles of writing are often identifiable, even to the casual reader. Some of the things you read may surprise you. You might even wonder if such things should be mentioned in a book like the Bible. Remember, the Holy Spirit expressed this message through real people, and their own feelings form part of God's message. This is a book about real people and real situations, written for real people and real situations.

Within the Bible there are also different types of literature. In the Old Testament there are some historical books (Genesis to Job). There is poetry (Psalms to Song of Songs). In addition there are the writings of prophets who addressed contemporary situations in their day (Isaiah to Malachi). Sometimes the culture and poetry of the Old Testament seem strange to modern readers. The prophets with their austere messages can be hard to come to terms with. However, once we begin to understand a little of the situation in which these books were formed, then they become relevant to our lives as we apply them.

The New Testament also contains a variety of literary forms. There is the history of the life of Jesus and of the early church (Matthew to Acts). There are letters from the Apostle Paul to churches scattered throughout the Roman empire (Romans to Philemon). There are also other letters written by people such as John and Peter (Hebrews to Revelation). The New Testament not only tells us about how Christianity was born, but shows us how the Old Testament can have relevance for Christians.

It is important when you begin reading the Bible, to have a good modern translation. The King James Version is certainly a magnificent translation but its archaic language can be difficult to understand. The New International Version is my personal favourite. It is an accurate, contemporary translation and is loved by many. The Good News and New American Standard versions are satisfactory alternatives. In the end it does not matter what version you have, so long as it is accurate and understandable.

Bible Study

Different people have different methods for reading and studying the Bible. Some prefer to read the Bible alongside some daily reading notes. These can certainly be of help, but for myself I just like to read the Bible on its own, thoughtfully, and noting down anything I learn as I go along. Using a notebook helps me to concentrate on what I am doing and ensures that I don't quickly forget what I have just read.

I find it helpful to ask questions as I read. Questions like:

What does this passage teach me about God?
What does this passage teach me about myself?
Is there a promise in this passage that I can hold on to?
Is there a warning for me?
Is there a command that I should follow?
Is there an example I could imitate?
In what way does this passage encourage me?

Reading the Bible with an enquiring mind is of great benefit. It is also good to pray both before and after reading the Bible. Beforehand ask God to speak to you clearly and when you have finished reading, ask God to help you remember and obey what you have just read. The Holy Spirit will play a vital role in helping you both to understand what you are reading and to apply it to your life. The Bible is not some kind of magic book, but if used prayerfully will have a transforming effect on our lives.

When I was a young Christian, someone advised me to read the entire contents of the Bible every year. I was told that if I read three chapters every day and five on a Sunday I would achieve this goal. Try though I may, I found it quite difficult to keep to this commitment (though I have read right through the Bible many times now). It is important to be realistic as well as disciplined when it comes to Bible reading. The Bible is a big book and many passages are very demanding. If you are going to find it impossible to read the whole Bible every year, then at least make sure you cover a substantial part of the Bible within more generous time limits (two years for example).

'Where is the best place to start?' This is a question I am often asked. If you haven't read much of the Bible, I would certainly recommend that you begin by reading one of the gospels. Mark's gospel in particular is quite brief and straight to the point. As an alternative John's gospel is worth considering. It was written with the purpose of convincing non-Christians of the deity of Jesus and contains many personal touches about his life.

After reading one of the gospels, it would be a good thing to read the 'Sermon on the Mount' found in Matthew chapters five to seven. This important section of teaching is a description of the lifestyle Jesus expects of his followers.

Next the book (letter) of James should be read. This very down to earth book covers a whole range of important and practical issues of Christian living. Just be warned as you read James; he has the habit of cutting right to the bone on many issues.

It would be worthwhile turning to one of Paul's

letters. Some of the letters Paul wrote are quite heavy going, for example the letter to the Romans. Colossians on the other hand is easy to read and very refreshing. It is a book that gives us a picture of Jesus in all his glory and stimulates us to worship him.

All of the Bible books I have mentioned so far are from the New Testament. I am often saddened to find that some Christians spend little time reading the Old Testament. Don't be afraid of it, for there are many important lessons that the Old Testament writers offer. Begin with Genesis and think about how God created the world and established a relationship with man.

In any Christian book shop you will find Bible reading programmes and study books that will help you in your understanding of the Bible. The important thing is to make sure that you do read the Bible regularly and with an open mind and heart so that God can speak to you and mould your thoughts and life. In the Appendix you will find a Bible reading programme that you might find useful. It does not cover the whole Bible, but includes extracts from every section of the Bible. If you wish to use it, you will get a flavour of the Bible as a whole, and that will be a good start.

PRAYER:
Father, thank you for revealing yourself to me through the Bible and for showing me how I should live my life.

Help me to read the Bible every day, and to discipline myself to study it so that I can grow as a Christian. Help me to live out the truth of your word and to be obedient to your commands. Amen.

Chapter 6

Our Enemy

As soon as someone becomes a Christian, his relationship with God is changed. The fact that Christians are able to call God, 'Father', is proof of this. But this is not the only relationship that changes. Satan is also aware of you becoming a Christian and is not pleased.

Who is Satan?
Who is Satan and why should we as Christians be concerned about him?

When God created the universe, he did not just create physical things, but spiritual beings also. The Bible talks about angels and demons, all of whom are part of the spirit world. All that God created was good (Gen. 1:31)! God was able to rejoice in all that he had made for it was a perfect creation. Despite this, we find a sinister character called Satan tempting Eve to sin (Gen. 3). Some time between creation and this event (which we call 'the fall') Satan must have changed; indeed sin must have come into being.

We read in various parts of the Bible that there was a great rebellion in Heaven (2 Pet. 2:4; Jude 6). A group of angels, puffed up with pride, attempted to overthrow God's rule and establish themselves as 'gods'. As punishment, these angels were expelled from God's presence and would forever be the enemies of God. Satan is the head of this group of fallen angels or demons and is the arch enemy of God. Indeed his very name means 'the Adversary'. His objective is to oppose God in any way he can, this is why he is the enemy of every Christian.

Though Satan has been condemned and expelled from God's presence, he still has tremendous power, and will use it to great effect. He is described as the *ruler of this world* (John 14:30), and the *prince of the power of the air* (Eph. 2:2). A quick glance at the state of present day society will reveal the extent of his evil work. Crime, immorality, greed, selfishness, perversion, witchcraft, injustice and depravity are all his hallmarks. There is no depth to which he will not stoop, no dirty trick he will not play in order to destroy God's creation.

Satan is not only the power behind corruption in society, but he also involves himself in the battle for the lives of individuals. At the very start of his career he tempted Eve to sin (Gen. 3). When Jesus came to free the world from sin, Satan tried to tempt him also (Matt. 4:1-11). On that occasion, Satan failed miserably.

He has not given up, however, for he continues to blind people to their spiritual need (2 Cor. 4:4). It may be that you knew about Christianity for a long time before you became a Christian. You were unconcerned about your future and lived complacently without giving a thought to your spiritual needs. That was Satan's work; he was blinding you in an attempt to keep you from the loving arms of God and the salvation he offers. God offers us life, peace and joy. Satan wants to rob us of these things and to take from God what is rightfully his.

There are two important things we need to know about Satan. Firstly he is the originator of all sin. We read in 1 John 3:8 that Satan sinned *from the beginning*, that is from the beginning of the creation. Even before Eve sinned, Satan was at work doing evil (2 Cor. 11:3). He is the *father of lies* (John 8:44), the one who invented wrong doing. God did not create anything sinful; he inspected his handiwork and saw that it was good. Satan, however, introduced sin into creation by rebelling against God. Ultimately all sin, rebellion, suffering, and death can be traced back to this most evil of creatures. Satan is, as his name suggests, the Adversary of all that is good.

Secondly it is important that you realise that Satan's power is limited. Evil though he may be, and powerful though he undoubtedly is, yet he remains no more than a creature who was brought into being by an almighty God. The Bible tells us that Satan can only do what God allows (Job 1:12). There is a boundary which God has set, and Satan cannot go beyond it. He can win battles but he will never win the war. He may hinder the work of God, but God will have the ultimate victory. Satan may mar lives, but God can heal them and forgive.

Resist the Devil
As God's children we too can be victorious over Satan. Indeed, if we resist him and stand firm in our

faith he will flee from us (James 4:7). It is important that we do this because he will never give up in his effort to destroy us and make us ineffective as Christians.

Some Christians are aware of Satan's power, but less aware of the power they have as God's children. They have developed an unhealthy obsession about Satan and as a result are leading defeated Christian lives. There are two great dangers – taking Satan too seriously and not taking him seriously enough. We need to make sure we get the balance right. Satan can do great harm to us and others, but he can also be overcome with God's help, if we are willing to put up a fight.

Now, how does Satan attack a Christian? If we are to successfully defend ourselves against him, we need to know what he is up to. The four main weapons in Satan's arsenal are accusation, deception, temptation and destruction.

The Accuser

In Revelation 12:10 Satan is described as the *Accuser*. We read that day and night Satan stands before God and accuses Christians. Not only does he accuse us before God but he also influences our minds, filling them with accusations.

To be fair, there is a great deal that we can be accused of. Think back to the kind of person you were before you became a Christian. I, for one, am ashamed of so many things that I said and did. Think also of your failures since becoming a Christian.

Think of the number of times you have let God down in some way. If we were to be honest we would probably have to confess that our Christian lives have been fairly mediocre at best.

Satan loves to remind us of what miserable failures we really are. He wants us to remember all the sins we committed before we were Christians. He whispers in our subconscious saying, 'How could someone as rotten as you become a Christian? Do you really think God loves you in spite of all that you have done?' As a result of these insinuations, many Christians are overwhelmed with guilt even after they have trusted Christ. This is Satan's dirty work.

Then he tries to remind us of the failures we commit each day as Christians. He whispers, 'Call yourself a Christian? No Christian would ever do what you have just done!' If we listen to his voice, we will begin to wonder if God really does love us. We will have grave doubts about the reality of our conversion and perhaps even wonder if it is worth continuing to follow Christ. These questions and doubts are both natural and common. It is Satan trying to discourage us from progressing as Christians.

How should we respond to such attacks? There are two things we must do. Firstly, we must remember that once a sin has been forgiven, it is finished with as far as God is concerned (Isa. 43:25). God doesn't forgive us one minute and then recall all our faults the next. God is our Father, he loves us and encourages us to go on, not wallow in our guilt. However difficult it may be to leave the past behind, we must do so. God has forgiven us, so we must forgive ourselves and go on serving him. If Satan reminds you of your past, remind him and yourself of the power of God's forgiveness.

The second thing we need to do is keep short accounts with God. Daily we must confess the sins that we are aware of and also ask forgiveness for the sins we have unknowingly committed. God is faithful to us and will always forgive, provided we genuinely repent of whatever we have done (1 John 1:9). Be open and honest with God when you pray. He is a loving Father and is well aware of your shortcomings. We need never feel guilty after we have confided in God.

The Deceiver

Not only does Satan try and accuse us, but he is also a *deceiver*. In his first contact with humanity, he deceived Eve into taking the forbidden fruit (Gen. 3). He is busily involved today deceiving Christians. We can be deceived in two ways. Firstly there is the deception of the mind. Satan would just love to fill our minds with falsehood, in an attempt to keep us from believing the truth. The fact that there are some 30,000 cults and false sects in existence today is testimony to his deceptive power.

We need to be careful not to be gullible. Even respected religious leaders have been used by Satan to deceive Christians. Martin Luther is once reputed to have said 'If you are looking for the Devil, make sure you search for him in the pulpit.' John in his day warned Christians about false teachers (1 John 4:1) and Paul also had to deal with the problem (1 Tim. 1:3). We must not allow our minds to be tainted by falsehood, but check everything by what the Bible says.

It is possible that Satan has already tried to shake your confidence in the Bible. Throughout the history of the church, people have attempted to attack the reliability of the Bible and declared it to be no more than a collection of stories. The constraints of this book would not permit me to argue a case for the reliability of the Bible, but let me just say that Christian scholars have for centuries been able to put their trust in the Bible without having to commit intellectual suicide. Beware of the deceptions that Satan would put in your way, and make sure that your mind is free from doubt.

The second kind of deception that Satan uses is deception of the heart. He loves to see Christians squandering their time, energy and resources on futile matters. Satan will try and convince you that true happiness can be found in money, sexual expression, social status or education. Some people will buy a new car thinking that it will make them more important in the eyes of society. Others will worship the god of science because they believe knowledge is the answer to the world's problems. Still others try to find fulfilment in a selfish and immoral lifestyle. In each case Satan has done his work of deception, distracting people from the most important thing in life, a relationship with God.

As Christians, we must keep our hearts pure and

be devoted to Christ and his kingdom. Only then will we be able to see beyond the superficiality of our age and resist the deceptive clutches of the adversary.

The Tempter

Satan is also a *Tempter*. We must never think of him merely as some animated character with a trident as the cartoons depict him, neither can we afford the luxury of believing him to be merely a mindless force of evil. Rather, he is a cunning and crafty being who knows all about our weaknesses and how to exploit them. Whether you struggle with sex, greed, money, power or some other vice, you can rest assured that he knows about it and will find plenty to tempt you with.

The Bible tells us to resist the Devil, but when it comes to temptation we are told to flee (2 Tim. 2:22). There is good reason for this advice. Temptation is at its strongest when the opportunity presents itself. The solution is simple. When you are tempted to do something you know to be wrong, get away from the situation and stay away.

I remember counselling a young Christian who had an addiction to pornographic literature. Most of the time he coped with his craving, but as soon as he went into a newsagent to get his paper, the sight of the magazines on the top shelf proved too much to cope with. He had spent many hours praying about his problem, but with every defeat his resolve weakened. For him the answer was never to go into the newsagent by himself. A simple solution, but one that has kept him safe ever since.

Not only do we need to remember to flee temptation, but it is also crucial that we do not allow the devil a foothold on our lives (Eph. 4:27). Any weakness, any vulnerability, any chance that we give him will be ruthlessly exploited. Watch out, be vigilant, and don't allow any lingering sin or weakness to take hold of your life. It will become a platform from which the Devil will launch his strikes.

The Destroyer
Finally the devil is a *Destroyer*. Peter put it well when he said, *Your enemy the devil prowls around like a roaring lion looking for someone to devour* (1 Pet. 5:8). I remember watching a nature programme about lions. One lioness was prowling in the long grass stalking an antelope. She crept close to her prey and waited patiently for an opportunity to strike. The antelope bowed its slender neck for a drink and suddenly found itself being savaged by the lioness. Within a few seconds it was all over.

Satan is patiently stalking you and me as Christians. He doesn't care how we fall, as long we do. He watches our every move closely, scrutinising us to find weaknesses. Once found, he will ensure that we are attacked at every vulnerable point, and, if possible, destroyed.

The apostle Paul was well aware of the ferocity of the devil's attacks, so he has painted a vivid picture for us of the defensive weapons at our disposal as Christians (Eph. 6:10-18). These weapons are known collectively as the Armour of God.

Ready for Battle

Even before Paul begins to describe the different components of this armour, he gives us three pieces of advice on spiritual warfare. Firstly we need to recognise that the battle is indeed spiritual. *Our struggle is not against flesh and blood ... but against spiritual forces of evil* (v. 12). Of course, Paul is not denying that we struggle on a human level, but behind the physical and tangible there are spiritual forces at work. The immorality of our society, false beliefs and philosophies, injustice, these are all evidence of Satan's power at work. This is a spiritual battle! Unless we realise the spiritual dimension, we will ultimately be unsuccessful.

Secondly we need to approach this battle with a positive attitude. Paul gives us the assurance that, *You can take your stand* (v. 11), provided we are well-equipped.

There is an account in 2 Kings 6 where the king of Aram went to war with Israel. God instructed Elisha the prophet where he should place his armies, and as a consequence they were prepared for every move the enemy made. The king of Aram got tired of constant defeat and so ordered his soldiers to go to the city of Dothan where Elisha was staying, and kidnap him.

When Elisha's servant went out of the city for a walk the next morning, he was terrified to see the city surrounded, and ran to tell his master. Upon hearing this distressing news Elisha calmly replied, that *those who are with us are more than those who are with them* (v. 16). In other words 'don't worry, anyone plus God is a majority'.

As Christians we need to realise that although the Devil is powerful, God is the most powerful being of all. This should give us confidence for the spiritual battle.

Thirdly, we need to be careful not to grow complacent. In verse 13 Paul says, *and after you have done everything, to stand.* In other words, our conflict with Satan will not just be a one-off battle, or even a few isolated skirmishes. This is a long, protracted war that begins the moment we trust Christ and will go on until the end of our lives. We need not become complacent with each victory; we must put the armour on and keep it on.

The Armour of God

The first piece of armour we have at our disposal is a belt. Paul describes this as a *belt of truth*. In those days soldiers wore loose fitting garments (rather like baggy T-shirts). It was very difficult to fight at close quarters with these clothes flapping everywhere, so soldiers wore a strong belt so that they could tuck these garments in and hold them securely.

The truth this belt represents is the truth of God's revelation, the Bible. It is obvious that if we are to successfully combat Satan we need a firm grasp of God's word. After all, how do we know what Satan is like, or the tactics he employs? How can we find the resources necessary to take a stand? He is a liar and a deceiver and wants to fill our minds with false ideas. How will we be able to distinguish lies from truth? The Bible will reveal all of these things to us, provided we give time to study.

The problem is, as I pointed out in the previous chapter, many Christians just don't read their Bibles. We cannot possibly hope to successfully take Satan on, unless we are adequately equipped with the knowledge found in the Bible. We need to take this issue seriously and not allow laziness to hold us back.

Next, Paul talks about the breastplate, which was a tough sleeveless piece of armour covering the torso, thus protecting the vital organs of the body. We are told that this *breastplate represents righteousness*. This can be understood in two ways. Firstly, God declares us to be righteous (or holy) because of the work of Christ. Satan cannot accuse us of our sin because we have been forgiven and are able to live with a clear conscience. Secondly, this can refer to the righteous life we live as Christians. Because we have been forgiven, we are motivated to live a holy life that pleases God. The very fact that we are obedient is in itself a great blow to Satan who tries to turn us against God.

We are then presented with what I like to call the *gospel boots*. Roman soldiers wore tough leather sandals which often had studs in the sole to give a better grip. These soldiers were therefore able to advance into enemy territory, confident of their footing. The implication is, that these boots are the ability God gives us to share our faith with other people. We know what the gospel of peace is, our lives have been changed by it and now we have something to share with the world.

How appropriate that evangelism is mentioned in this passage dealing with spiritual warfare. There is nothing Satan fears more than Christians who are determined to tell others about Jesus and the salvation he offers. Satan is afraid of the contagious effect this message has. If we want to see Satan defeated, his kingdom crumbling while the kingdom of God grows, then just keep witnessing. As we tell others about Jesus, and they too respond to this message, so we drive forcibly into Satan's territory.

You can be sure he doesn't like it. He will try anything he can to stop Christians witnessing and to a great extent he is successful because 95% of Christians never lead another person to Christ. But as long as we keep witnessing and see people make decisions to follow Christ, we keep Satan on the defensive.

Paul then talks about the *shield of faith*. Roman soldiers used shields which were about 4½ feet high and 2½ feet wide. They would stand in a long line (known as a phalanx), linking all their shields together to form a solid wall of defence. This tells us two things about our faith. Firstly, if our faith is genuine, then no part of our body is left exposed to Satan's fiery darts. Secondly, our faith when joined with the faith of other Christians is a potent force. As Christians we can encourage each other and help one another to be strong.

As Satan throws his flaming darts of fear and

discouragement at us, by faith we can affirm our confidence in Christ. He is alive, he loves us, he is faithful, and he will never be defeated. We can stand up to these attacks of Satan by believing that Christ is in control of our lives and has our best interests at heart.

Next comes the helmet of salvation. In 1 Thessalonians 5:8 Paul talks about *the hope of salvation as a helmet*. This piece of armour is not just concerned about our situation now, but also our future. Without hope in the future, life now is pretty pointless. All that we do now as Christians would be in vain if there is no promise of heaven.

Whatever setbacks we might suffer in this great battle, whatever difficulties we have to endure, we have the certain hope that our destiny is secure, and there is something far more wonderful than this life to look forward to. This eternal perspective will revolutionise our outlook on life and enable us to endure anything, for there is more for us than this life alone can offer.

Finally there is the *sword of the Spirit*. The sword of the spirit is the word of God, the Bible. We have already thought of the Bible as a means of protection; now we need to think of it as a means of attack.

We read in Hebrews 4:12 that the word of God is *sharper than a two edged sword*. It has the ability to cut to the bone and give God's judgment on any situation. As we look over a world that is torn apart by sin, a world of injustice, immorality, inequality and corruption, we can launch an offensive with the word of God. When we condemn evil, we do not do so on our own authority, but on the very authority of God. When the Bible is used, there is no argument or ambiguity. God's word is the final authority, and even Satan with all his demonic might is powerless to do anything about that.

Therefore, we condemn evil with confidence. We take our stand against the wrongs of this world knowing that although Satan is opposing us, yet we speak in God's name, and the final victory will be ours. We must wield the sword of the Spirit skilfully and appropriately, and this requires a good knowledge of its content. When we do so, we go into battle as soldiers who are equipped for anything.

PRAYER:

Father, thank you that you want the very best for me because you love me. Thank you that Jesus on the cross conquered Satan and that I too can have victory over Satan in my life.

Protect me from Satan's accusations, from his deceitful lies and help me to resist his temptations.

Thank you for the armour you provide me with: the Bible, the righteousness which Christ gives me, the ability to tell others about you, the shield of faith and the helmet of my salvation. Help me to use this armour every day so that I can experience spiritual victory. Help me always to be prepared for Satan's attacks. Amen.

Chapter 7

Salty and Shining

'If there is a God then why is the world in such a mess?' This question was put to me by a young man with whom I was trying to share my faith. The point he raised is a very important one. If God exists then surely he must be concerned about all the bad things that are occurring in the world, and he must have the power to bring about change for the better.

In response to this question I pointed out two things. Firstly, if God were to rid the world of all wrong he would have to wipe out humanity, for the seeds of evil exist in all of our lives. Secondly, God is concerned and is doing something about the state of the world. Not only did God send Jesus to die for our sin, but he continues to work through Christians to change society for the better.

Jesus talked about Christians being Salt and Light (Matt. 5:13-16). These two metaphors are not as meaningful in our day as they were at the time of Jesus. In the days before freezers, salt was rubbed into meat as a preservative. Its presence in the meat would slow the processes of decay, keeping the meat fresh for longer. Salt was also used to make food taste better. Even if the food was pretty tasteless to begin with, the presence of salt would at least make it palatable.

As Christians we have the job of making society

a better place. Our presence should have a preserving effect on our homes and communities. It is hard to imagine a society where justice and equity are commonplace and where Christian values are the norm. Our present society is so corrupt and rotten already, that any change for the better may seem impossible. However, we as Christians are salt; we have no choice in the matter, for this is what being a Christian is all about. We should, therefore, make a difference and make life more palatable for people, and we will provided we remain salty. In other words, maintain our distinctive character as described in a passage which we call the Beatitudes (Matt. 5:1-12).

The Happy Life

In this passage Jesus uses the word *blessed* or *happy* on nine occasions. We should not think of this merely as a subjective emotion, Jesus is not just talking about a good feeling someone has when things are going well for him. This person is blessed or happy because God recognises the value of his actions. The situations described are from God's perspective not man's.

Humanly speaking, we equate happiness with material prosperity, security, success in business, or achievement in some way or other. If someone is well off, has a secure job, a good house, a family, and all the modern comforts that money can buy, then we would consider him to be fortunate or blessed. This is not necessarily how God views him. Jesus makes eight statements about people who are blessed.

The Poor in Spirit

Blessed are the poor in spirit, said Jesus, *for theirs is the kingdom of heaven* (v. 3). The mention of the word 'spirit' infers that Jesus was not talking primarily about material poverty. In the Old Testament someone who was 'poor' was a person who recognised that he was unable to save himself and therefore totally dependant upon God for salvation (Isa. 41:17,18). He had nothing to offer God, so he threw himself at God's mercy recognising how unworthy he was. This kind of person, according to Jesus, is the one to whom the kingdom of God will be given.

God will not allow the proud or the self-righteous to enter his kingdom. Anyone who feels he has a right to eternal life will not get it. Only those who recognise humbly that they are nothing, will be allowed to form part of God's kingdom. This, of course, contrasts with our society where people carry over-inflated ideas of their own worth and believe that they deserve nothing but the best (in addition to blessings from God if they believe he exists).

Those who Mourn

Next Jesus blesses *those who mourn, for they will be comforted* (v. 4). How can we equate happiness with mourning? These people who mourn do so because they recognise sin in their own lives and are deeply troubled by it. This is a development of the first statement Jesus made. It is one thing to recognise that you are an unworthy sinner, it is another matter to feel deeply troubled and sorry for your sin. Only those who repent in this way can experience the comfort of God's forgiveness.

In our society we see many people who don't care about the wrongs they commit. The terrorist is unmoved by the suffering and anguish he has caused. The business man does not care when his ruthlessness leads to the exploitation of others. Even the politician can support an immoral law or policy without blushing at its consequences. As Christians we do care and are heartbroken whenever we sin. We have, however, the consolation that our repentance brings us closer to God.

The Meek
Blessed are the meek, said Jesus *for they will inherit the earth* (v. 5). Meekness has got nothing to do with weakness or timidity, rather it is exercising a self-control, enabling us to be humble, gentle and courteous. In that sense a very strong person can be meek. As Christians we recognise our shortcomings and the fact that God accepts us in spite of them. The result is that we treat other people in the same gentle manner in which God treats us.

In our society, people learn to stand up for themselves. If someone is offended they look for an opportunity to get revenge and to hurt the other person more than they themselves have been hurt. Our society believes in the survival of the fittest, but Jesus taught that might is not right, and went further by saying that might will never inherit the earth. Only the meek have God on their side and only they can be confident of an eventual reward.

Those who Hunger and Thirst for Righteousness
Jesus went on to talk about those who *hunger and thirst after righteousness* (v. 6). Hunger and thirst are about the most basic human instincts. As Christians we should not only mourn our sin but also crave a positive righteousness. Being righteous not only means having a right relationship with God but also living the kind of life that pleases God. Our motives, actions and speech should all indicate that we are living righteous lives. When we have a healthy appetite for this kind of lifestyle then we will 'be filled'. God will reward us for the life we lead, both in this life by giving us spiritual contentment, and in the next.

Our society does not have the same kind of appetite. It seems to me that people have an appetite for things that are destructive, like selfishness, moral filth, exploitation or dishonesty. These wrong desires may be fed but they will never be satisfied. People who cherish wrong appetites are destined to live lives that are empty and unfulfilled. Only the life that God offers can be truly fulfilling; this is the life for which God created us.

The Merciful
Jesus went on to say, *Blessed are the merciful for they will be shown mercy* (v. 7). Mercy is compassion for people who are in need. It is a deep, practical,

caring concern which extends well beyond a pious sympathy. This mercy can be shown to anyone who is in need. Mercy was perfectly expressed in the life of Jesus. Whenever he saw hungry people he fed them, when he came across the diseased leper he healed him. When Jesus saw people who were aimless and without hope he felt compassion for them.

Our society has little time for the weak. It is true that we have a social security system which provides a safety net for those who are in trouble, but in general few are willing to lend a helping hand to the helpless. The strong are allowed to get stronger, while the helpless become increasingly more helpless. The Christian should not focus his attention on those who are successful in life, rather he should care for the wounded and the lonely. In showing mercy to others, we in turn are shown mercy by God who sees all things.

Pure in Heart

Next Jesus talked about the *pure in heart* (v. 8). This is not just a moral purity, but a single-minded loyalty to God (Deut. 6:5). One translation describes this person as 'utterly sincere'. The person's thoughts, motives and actions are fully consistent with his devotion to God.

It is an easy thing to play at religion. Some claim to have a faith, but it seems to desert them the moment they step out of a church building and into the world outside. To such people religion is just a Sunday activity. To the Christian God is his life. All that he does, thinks and says should reflect his love for God.

What is the reward for having a pure heart? *They will see God.* God will be found if we are prepared to seek him (Jer. 29:13). As we focus our minds on God and devote our lives to him he will reveal himself to us and lead us into an intimate relationship with him.

The Peacemakers

Blessed are the peacemakers, for they will be called sons of God (v. 9). This beatitude implies that all Christians are to be peacemakers, striving to bring about reconciliation wherever we are. God himself is the great peacemaker (Eph. 2:14-18) so it is not surprising that if we are to be in the peace business, we need to reflect the character of our Father God.

Coming as I do from Northern Ireland, I am well aware of the damage that conflict can cause. As a nurse I saw people who were physically wounded and even killed, because of the enmity between opposing sides. But there were more than just physical wounds; whole communities were seething with hatred and fear because of the invisible but potent wall of sectarianism that imprisoned them.

There was a great wall that divided us from God and from each other. Through the work of the Cross Jesus removed this dividing wall and made reconciliation between God and man possible. As Christians we are to bring this atmosphere of calm with us wherever we are. In a society where conflict is commonplace, we are to be an influence for reconciliation and hope. In families that are broken apart by strife we are to soothe wounds and encourage peace and forgiveness.

Those persecuted because of Righteousness
And finally, *Blessed are those who are persecuted because of righteousness, for theirs is the kingdom of heaven* (v. 10). With all the qualities Jesus mentioned, it is strange to think that Christians could be persecuted. Why harm someone who is doing nothing but good?

Jesus himself experienced suffering because of righteousness. His life was lived selflessly for the good of mankind and yet he was crucified by the very people he was trying to save. Why the paradox?

Our society likes conformity. It feels uncomfortable when someone is different. All the qualities mentioned in the beatitudes are the opposite of our society's values. To be Christlike is to be a rebel. We as Christians are the most radical revolutionaries the world has seen. It is hardly surprising that society finds it hard to appreciate us. When we are rejected, when the values we preach are ignored, we should rejoice because that is evidence in itself that we are doing the will of God. Those' who do the will of God, according to Jesus, will inherit the Kingdom.

Salt and Light
Being salt, therefore, means to live as Jesus lived, not following the crowd but being positively

different. In our society pride, selfishness, and hypocrisy are the norm. The weak are all too often exploited while the strong aggressively assert their influence on those they can control. The Christian is to be humble, recognising that he is nothing without God. He is to live a holy life, devoted to God and to caring for his fellow man. He is to be a servant in a world where everyone wishes to be a master and his ambition is to care for the needs of others before ever demanding his own rights.

This seems to be an impossibly high standard to attain. But salt is what we are! Jesus never promised that the Christian life would be easy, but he did assure us that we would never have to live it alone for he would always be with us (Matt. 28:20). The Holy Spirit, too, fulfils a vital role in the equation. It is through the work of the Spirit in our lives that we are transformed to become like Jesus. This transformation begins at conversion and continues throughout our Christian lives. The salt is already there, it simply needs divine power coupled with a willingness on our part to surrender daily to the work of the Holy Spirit, in order to be effective.

Jesus talked about salt losing its saltiness (v. 13). When this happens it becomes pretty useless. Strictly speaking pure salt cannot lose its salinity, but Jesus was talking about the impure salt that was dug up from the Dead Sea. If the actual sodium chloride within the salt dissolved, only a useless gritty residue would remain. As Christians we need to retain our purity and Christ-like character, otherwise we are of no value to the society around us, and we will never be able to influence it for good.

Next, Jesus talked about light which has a similar but complementary function. Light expels darkness, making the way ahead visible. Wherever light shines, it makes a difference. The darkness is altered and will remain so for as long as the light is shining brightly. Jesus described this light as *good works* (Matt. 5:16). As we do good works so our light shines brightly. These good works are the things that we do and say because we are Christians. We are changed people, and this change should manifest itself in our behaviour towards others.

We have already been thinking about the kind of society we live in. Lies and deceit are common and it is the done thing to cheat, to be selfish and to live without any concern for others. As Christians we cannot live like this for we must model our lives on Jesus. In doing so we will stick out like a 'sore thumb', or rather like a brightly shining light. We expose the sin that is all around us and show others an example to follow. Salt preserves and makes life more palatable, light exposes sin and demonstrates how people should live. As Christians we will be lights to this dark world provided we can remain bright.

It is interesting to note as we look at church history, that Christians have often been at the forefront of positive changes in society. Slavery was abolished in Britain because Christians like William Wilberforce actively campaigned against it. Dr. Tom

Barnardo, George Muller and Charles Spurgeon were well known Christian leaders who opened up orphanages to care for Britain's abandoned children. Around the world today, Christians are feeding the hungry, clothing the naked, healing the sick, and caring for the poor, in addition to campaigning on a wide variety of moral issues. They are selflessly living for the good of others, to make this world a better, more humane place.

The motive behind all of these actions is clear. They, and many other Christians, have devoted their lives to being salt and light. They have endeavoured to make our society more just, and a more acceptable place to live in. Such ideals stem not from an arid religious existence, but from a life-changing encounter with Jesus Christ which refines us and gives us a compassion for the world around us.

Be Different

These metaphors of salt and light teach us four important things about our responsibility as Christians in the world. Firstly, the Christian should be distinctly different from his non-Christian neighbour. Jesus compared light with darkness, we might make the comparison between chalk and cheese. While it is true that non-Christians can be kind and generous while some Christians behave in a disgraceful way, yet Jesus makes the assumption that we as Christians *are* different. This puts a responsibility upon us to *be* different, both in our actions and speech. Our very motives need to be selfless so that we learn to serve others before we serve ourselves. Our lives and conduct should be so modelled on Jesus that if others begin to imitate what we are doing they would be indirectly imitating him.

Don't Lose it

Secondly, we must make sure that we do not lose this distinctiveness. Sin can so easily dominate our lives and render us ineffective. We can compromise, and in so doing blend in with the sinful standards of the world. Fear of what other people might say or think about us could so easily prevent us from standing up for what is right. Even apathy can become a problem as we opt out of our responsibility for the sake of an easy life. The only way to be truly effective in society is to be distinctly different – so salty that people can't but help notice, so bright that we cannot be ignored. We need to radiate the very character of Jesus by all that we do, say or even think. Only then will we be able to influence the world around us, by halting the spread of evil and promoting truth, love and compassion.

Be Effective

Thirdly, we need to be effective. I remember once rinsing my mouth with salt water to get rid of some infected ulcers. My mouth was stinging so much it almost brought tears to my eyes. Salt has that kind of effect, and clearly Jesus expected Christians to exert a similarly piercing influence on society. During his lifetime Jesus condemned many of the wrongs in society, especially the religious hypocrisy of the Pharisees. Some of the things he said to them were harsh, though well deserved, calling them *whitewashed tombs full of decay* (Matt. 23:27) and *sons of hell* (Matt. 23:15). In the same way we as Christians need to be courageous and outspoken in condemning evil. Whether on the factory floor, in school or at social gatherings, we need to speak up when wrong is being done.

When there is gossip, don't take part, rather defend whoever is being slated. If business colleagues are dishonest, always tell the truth and stand up for what is right. When we see someone being victimised, step in to help. If the conversation and jokes are obscene, take a moral stance. When people tell us that we are being intolerant if we don't accept abortion or homosexuality, then we must stand our ground and be prepared for the jibes. Whatever the cost we must continue to fight the decay that is occurring all around us, and defend what is true, for this is what it means to be salt and light.

Get Involved

Fourthly, we must be involved in the lives of people around us. As long as salt remains in its salt cellar, it will never flavour anything. Likewise a candle that is covered up will never pierce darkness. It goes without saying that if we are to be effective in our world, we need to be where the people are. There is such a temptation for Christians to spend so much time together that they never spend time with the very people who need salt and light. Churches can so easily become fortresses, giving security to those in the church while keeping everyone else away.

There are many Christians who don't have even one non-Christian friend. Jesus was once accused (quite rightly) of mixing with known sinners. It was, of course, his intention to move in circles where he could be an influence for good. This is an important lesson for the church. We must be involved in society if we are ever to change it. Do not feel that now you are a Christian you cannot have meaningful relationships with non-Christian friends. You can, and by living a holy life before them, you can demonstrate what Christianity is all about.

PRAYER:
Father, thank you that you want to change the world rather than destroy it. Thank you for the example Jesus left of someone who was holy and loving.

Help me to follow him by being salt and light in my family, neighbourhood and work place. I ask that I will be able to live a life that will influence others for good and prove that my faith is real. Amen.

Chapter 8

All Together Now

When asked to describe the word 'church', one young boy replied, 'Church is where well dressed people go to listen to a man talking for a very long time. They don't get up because if they stay long enough they get some bread and Ribena at the end.' Though a childish description, this comment is a reminder of the fact that many people, even Christians, have not really grasped the meaning of the word 'church'. For some, church is an exclusive religious club, for others it is a particular type of building. We associate it with formality, good clothes, respectability and authority. But is this what church is really all about?

A Definition

Even before the word 'church' appeared in the New Testament, it was used in the secular world. The Greek word *ekklesia* (from which we get our word 'ecclesiastical') simply meant 'a meeting that had been called' or 'a summoned assembly'. In the Greek city-states of the ancient world, a form of democracy was practised with every citizen having a say in public affairs. Town criers would call people to a public place where a debate would take place.

The Early Church

The church in the New Testament era appeared to have little by way of organisation. For a start there were no special buildings for their meetings. The Christians in Jerusalem did attend the Temple, but when they shared communion together they preferred the intimate surroundings of a home. This appears to have been standard practice. We must also note that there were no denominational structures like we have today. I often wonder how those first century Christians would cope if they were to join one of our twentieth century churches!

For these Christians the word 'church' was used in two ways. Firstly, it was any group of Christians who met together in a particular locality. These groups or churches were autonomous and would have been, for the most part, small tightknit communities. Each church would have been led by a group of elders (bishops) who were supported by deacons. Though there was no governing body supervising the activities of these local churches, there was communication between them, with leaders like Paul providing a point of reference for them. Each church considered itself accountable to God, but in fellowship with other churches.

Secondly the word church was used to refer to the universal community of believers. In this sense every Christian throughout the world was part of the church, with Christ as the head. Each local group, no matter how small, represented the church at large. This great truth gave significance and responsibility to every church, wherever it was.

Fellowship

One of the important words used by early Christians was the word 'fellowship'. This word also had its uses in secular life. It literally meant 'to share' of 'to have in common'. It could have been used of business partners who shared the same financial interests, or of a married couple who shared their marriage together. For Christians there was so much common ground to celebrate. They may have come from different nations and cultural backgrounds, but they shared a common faith (Titus 1:4). God had called each Christian into fellowship with Jesus (1 Cor. 1:9) and this meant that all Christians were bound together by more than mere shared opinions; they were joined by a supernatural tie that defied racial and cultural boundaries.

In Ephesians 2:19 Paul talks about God's household. We as Christians are a community, so linked, that the word 'foreigner' cannot exist among us. There are no strangers, no outcasts, no one is unwelcome. Anyone who is a Christian has the right to call another Christian 'brother', and expect to be treated as such.

A comparison between the New Testament church and the church of today could hardly be more stark. The formality of many of our church services, the denominational divisions which seem at times impregnable, the hierarchical systems of church government we have developed, would all be alien to our first century counterparts. Church is not about dressing up on a Sunday, it is not about elaborate buildings, committees or timetables. The church is a community of Christians who wish to share their lives together because of a common love and commitment to Jesus Christ, the supreme head of the church.

Misunderstandings about the nature of the church have caused many Christians to give importance to things which are simply not important; the buildings in which we meet, for example. Up until the end of the second century there were no specially constructed buildings for worship. Now buildings themselves are sometimes given a greater status than they deserve. Some churches spend vast fortunes on buildings which, though beautiful, are of little practical value. One church I know refused to allow its youth clubs to use the new building in case the young people did any damage. What can be more absurd than a building taking priority over the needs of the people in the church? Perhaps we need to question the spending of vast amounts of money on buildings if they are only used for a couple of hours on a Sunday and an hour or so midweek.

Traditions, too, can be given an importance well beyond their value. Inevitably certain practices performed regularly by our churches will become institutionalised and therefore part of tradition. Some of these will be useful and constructive, but some harmful. For example, despite the flourishing creativity of modern Christian song writers, many churches insist on using songs of a previous generation as the norm in their worship services. There are, of course, many great hymns of the past that are meaningful and powerful today, but if these are used continually rather than occasionally, we are in danger of conducting services which are past their 'sell-by' date.

The church is the living, breathing community of faith. It should never become a calcified or stagnant institution. Neither should we lose sight of our calling and purpose, to live as God's children in a dying world, caring for one another, worshipping our Saviour and serving those who are still outside of the church.

The Bible uses two important metaphors to describe what the church should be like. The church is a family and a body. In John 1:12 we read, *yet to all who receive him ... he gave the right to become children of God.* Families exist because God designed human beings to live in families. The family is the basic unit of society. How appropriate that a group of Christians, with so much in common, should be seen as a family.

The Family

We noted in chapter one that popular saying, 'You can choose your friends but not your family'. This of course is true of the church family as well as our blood relations. It is impossible to find the perfect church because every church is made up of failing individuals like you and me. In all probability, if you belong to a church, there will be some members that you find it difficult to get along with. They may be struggling to get on with you as well. There will be some people in your church that you would never have formed a friendship with but for the fact that you are both Christians; they would not be your natural choice for a friend.

Be that as it may, every member of your church is a member of your family. They are your brother and sister, and whether you like it or not, it is your job to love them and share your life with them. You and they are all children of God and members of his family.

Favouritism

In every family there are problems, and the church family is no exception. Take the problem of favouritism for example. Within many families there are favourites. A favourite parent, son, daughter, brother or sister. Favouritism is very damaging because it leads to feelings of rejection and isolation on the part of those family members who are not favourites.

Within the church it is possible to have favourites. I know one church where the youth leader showed favouritism to a couple of the young people in his care. If ever problems occurred, these two young folk were never blamed; as far as the youth leader was concerned they could do no wrong. Needless to say, this caused a great deal of hurt.

In another situation, a group of friends within a church formed a clique which was exclusive to their inner circle. The result was that some people within that church had to sit by themselves during every service and were never invited to birthdays and other social gatherings. This too caused serious hurts.

Why does favouritism occur? I believe that favouritism is a conscious decision a person makes about who is valuable to him and who is not. We decide to esteem some people and to ignore others. On one occasion the disciples made such a choice (Mark 10:13-14). Jesus had been very busy teaching and performing miracles. The disciples were enjoying being with the 'Master' and were feeling rather flattered that they were important enough to be chosen by Jesus. Earlier Jesus had felt the need to challenge their pride with a powerful illustration (Mark 9:33-37).

Some people approached this little band in the hope that Jesus would bless their children. The disciples were angry and tried to get rid of them. This was a bad mistake, bearing in mind the lesson Jesus had just taught them. In their minds the disciples had made a value judgment. They considered each other much more important than these children. Surely Jesus would have no time for a bunch of noisy kids! How wrong they were.

Jesus showed no favouritism. To him small children were just as important as adults. They were not to be left out or ostracised. True, children did not occupy a significant place in society, but, said Jesus, *the Kingdom of God belongs to such as these* (v. 14).

We must learn that within the church, all men, women and children are equal under God. We are all his children. As soon as we make judgments about who is important and who is not, we are sinning. If we show favouritism by the way we behave towards others, we offend God. You may well find that there are some people in your church that you are particularly drawn to. You find them witty, easy to talk to, attractive. There is nothing wrong with that But you need to care for everyone in the church and consider each person to be of equal value. It is vital that our churches are a haven for all and that no one is ever excluded.

Criticism

Another problem within families is criticism. Often our harshest words are reserved for our family members. We say things to them that we would not dare say to anyone else. I suppose this is because we are so familiar with the people in our families that we take them for granted.

Criticism stems from an unwillingness to accept people for who they are. I can remember times in my own family when I was very critical of my brothers. Whatever they did, they would feel the sharpness of my tongue. Even if they did the same things I was doing, yet I would still find reason to criticize them.

Some people are never happy with anyone or anything. They are always complaining and critical. This kind of attitude should have no place in the Christian church. Criticism comes so easily to many of us. We are tempted to criticize fellow Christians, our church leaders, and anyone who does not do what we want. Criticism stems from an unwillingness to love and accept each other, and it will divide our church, embittering its members.

Jesus, ever aware of the potential conflicts between believers, urged his listeners not to judge, or condemn, but to forgive (Luke 6:37). Within the church we need to practise what Jesus taught and be very careful about what we say to or about each other. It is important to be constructive and see the good in each other as well as the bad. Most important of all we need to learn to accept each other, whatever our faults, and in doing so build solid relationships.

Selfishness

Yet another common family problem is selfishness. I suppose there is that element in all of us that thinks that everyone else exists to fulfil our personal needs. We expect other people to fit in with our plans while at the same time we are not willing to make the same kind of sacrifices.

A friend of mine has recently left home and is beginning to discover just how much he took his family for granted. He always expected his mother to cook and clean for him as well as tidy up everything. His father was there to supply the money and security he needed. Younger brothers and sisters were always expected to concede whenever there was an argument. Two weeks into his newly found independence, he had begun to discover that living in student digs was not quite as accommodating as home. He suddenly realised that his relationship with his family had been about give and take. They gave and he took!

HAMILTON COLLEGE LIBRARY

Sometimes people approach the church with that view. They believe that the church's sole purpose is to supply their needs. It is true that the church should be caring, and that our church life should centre around the needs of people. But each individual has a responsibility to contribute to the life of the church as well as benefit from membership.

Too many people have said to me, 'I don't get enough out of going to church?' My reply is, 'Well what are you contributing to the life of your church?' Every church does have its problems, some more than others, but the answer is not to sit back and complain. Changes and improvements will only come when each person plays his part and makes a contribution to the whole.

Jesus said, *I am the good shepherd. The good shepherd lays down his life for the sheep* (John 10:11). When Jesus came to earth, it was not to be a king but a servant. He lived to enrich the lives of others. His humility was such that he even washed the dusty feet of his own disciples (John 13:5). Finally in one great act of sacrifice, he died an agonizing death on the cross, so that you and I could be blessed. This is our example! We should serve one another and be prepared to make sacrifices so that others are blessed. To misquote a famous line, 'ask not what your church can do for you, but what can you do for your church'.

The Body

Another metaphor which the Bible uses to describe the church is that of a body (1 Cor. 12:12-26). The human body is a wonderful and fascinating unit, and has a multitude of component parts, each of which is quite different from all the others.

The church is a collection of very different individuals, and yet at the same time it is one body, the body of Christ.

Growing Together

The use of the word 'body' to describe the church challenges us with some important lessons. Firstly, if a body is to remain healthy, then all the parts of the body must grow together. As Christians we should never become spiritually static. The Christian life is all about learning, developing and becoming more like Jesus. As we make ourselves available to the Holy Spirit, he moulds us into the kind of people God wants us to be.

The church as a whole should be growing as well, not just numerically but spiritually also. Of course the two are linked. As the church is made up of individuals, so it can only grow when its members grow. A church will only progress if its members are progressing. Each person within the church therefore has a responsibility for the spiritual health of the whole. We each have a responsibility to grow.

I remember once seeing a child whose body was growing, apart from his arms. It was a sad sight because that child would never really be healthy. The rest of his body would have to compensate for the lack in his arms.

Some churches are like that. They rely on the strength of just a few of the members, while the majority remain spiritually stunted. The weaker members are quite happy to rely on the strength of the few, but they do not realise that their weakness is hampering the progress of the body as a whole. They are receiving and being supported, but are making no real contribution.

In many churches, twenty percent of the membership is doing ninety percent of the work. This is not how a healthy body should be. Each individual needs to feel the responsibility for the body as a whole.

Significant

Secondly, if the body is to remain healthy, each part needs to recognise its own significance. It may well be that at the moment you don't feel as if you are a significant member of your church. Perhaps you look at those members of your church who have a very up-front role, speakers or in some leadership capacity, and you feel that they have a more important contribution to make than you. If this is the case, then prepare yourself for a shock. You are as important to the life of your church as anyone.

We make a great mistake in assuming that those who have a public role in the church are the most important. This is simply not the case. Yes, their role may be different from yours, but not more important.

To illustrate this point, Paul told a humorous parable (v. 15, 16).

> *If the foot should say, 'Because I am not a hand, I do not belong to the body,' it would not for that reason cease to be part of the body. And if the ear should say, 'Because I am not an eye, I do not belong to the body,' it would not for that reason cease to be part of the body.*

Suppose your foot had a mind of its own and felt jealous of your hand with its great dexterity and slender fingers, yet this would not make the foot any less a part of the body. Four hands and no feet would certainly be a disadvantage to the body. The ear does not have the ability to see things, but we would be much the poorer if we could not hear anything. Each and every part of the body has its place and function.

A number of years ago during my nursing days, an old man was admitted for surgery on his gangrenous feet. In the end the surgeons only had to remove four toes, including his two big ones. Much to his surprise, when the treatment was complete, the man realised that walking was suddenly difficult. Our toes, unimportant though they may seem, actually balance the body and prevent it from falling forward. It took extensive physiotherapy and a special pair of shoes before he was walking norm-ally again. Just toes, but none the less an important part of the body.

God has designed the church with you in mind. It would not be complete without you and will never function adequately unless you play a full part. True, we will all have different roles, but each role is important. It may take some time before you can find a way of contributing to the church, you may even have to ask advice from some of your church leaders. You must, however, ensure that you get involved within your church, so that others can be blessed through what you are doing.

Need Each Other

Thirdly, Paul emphasized that if the body is to be healthy we have to recognise that we need each other (v. 21).

> *The eye cannot say to the hand, 'I don't need you!'*
> *And the head cannot say to the feet, 'I don't need you.'*

If the whole body were an eye it would not be much good. It could see well, but would be unable to react to what it had seen!

The church is not about one-man armies. As Christians, we need to remember that we form one body. God designed it that way so that we could be of help to one another and give mutual support.

Paul was one of the most gifted Christians ever. Yet he never worked alone. Wherever he went, he took companions with him, men like Barnabas, Silas, Luke and Timothy. They were as much part of his life as he was of theirs. This model of teamwork should be adopted in our church lives.

Don't be afraid to ask your fellow Christians for help. They are there for you. Neither should you feel threatened when someone in your Church gives you advice. We are a body and there should be the kind of trusting atmosphere that makes openness possible.

No church is perfect because it is made up of failing individuals like you and me. But the church is a family and a body. You are God's gift to your church, and the members of your church are a gift to you. Get involved! Play your part, and you will begin to discover just how important the church can be in your life.

PRAYER:
Father, thank you for providing me with a family; brothers and sisters who will love me and care for me. Thank you that you express yourself through the church, the body of Christ.

Help me not to be critical of the faults I see in my church, but to be constructive and play my part. Help me to grow, so that the body as a whole can grow. I want to be a help, not a burden. Give me the strength and the wisdom to be a blessing to my fellow Christians. Amen.

Chapter 9

Gifts and Giving

Every member of the church is important. God wants to use all of us to build his church, and see it mature. But what can we do to achieve this? How will we equip ourselves for this great task?

Once again we want to think about the work of the Holy Spirit. Not only does the Holy Spirit make it possible for us to have a relationship with God, he also instils within us Christ-like character. But there is another role that the Holy Spirit plays in our lives. This role has less to do with his activity *in* our lives, and more to do with his working *through* us.

I refer to the Holy Spirit's role in preparing Christians for service. As the Holy Spirit works in our lives, he gives us a desire to serve Christ and his church, and the equipment to perform whatever service Christ wants of us. This equipment is referred to in the Bible as 'Spiritual Gifts'.

Spiritual Gifts

A spiritual gift is not quite the same as a natural ability, though the two are sometimes related. All human beings are made in the image of God (Gen. 1:26) and therefore all have certain natural abilities. For example, I have a friend who is very talented in music. Not only does he play the piano beautifully, he just needs to hear a tune once and can instantly reproduce it on his piano with precision. This talent is wonderful, I get very jealous every time I hear him play, but it has nothing to do with the fact that he is a Christian. Indeed, before he became a Christian he played the piano just as well. Even atheists can be musical!

Spiritual gifts, on the other hand, are exclusive to Christians. They and they alone can exercise them. It is only when a person becomes a Christian that the Holy Spirit can work through him in this way, empowering him to serve Christ and the church.

It is the spiritual gifts which make it possible for us to serve God effectively. They enable failing and weak people like you and me to work powerfully, doing things which we would not be capable of doing in our own strength. This is God's way of working through us. By giving us spiritual gifts, he enables us to play our part in his work.

Although spiritual gifts and fruits are distinct, they are also related. Spiritual gifts are useless without fruit. Take the fruit of love as an example. In 1 Corinthians 13:1-3, Paul clearly states that a person who was very gifted would nonetheless be useless if he did not demonstrate the fruit of love in his life. Spiritual gifts are not a short-cut to a powerful and dynamic spiritual life. There is no point asking for spiritual gifts if you are not prepared to take the difficult pathway towards spiritual maturity. Rather, spiritual gifts enable a disciple of Jesus Christ not just to experience the power of the Holy Spirit in his life, but also to harness that power and channel it into effective Christian service.

There is one last distinction we need to make. Spiritual gifts are not the same as Christian obligations. We read in 1 Corinthians 12:9 about the gift of faith, but the Bible also tells us that without faith it is impossible to please God (Heb. 11:6). Ephesians 4:11 talks about the gift of an evangelist whereas Acts 1:8 infers that all Christians are witnesses for Christ. What is the difference between a Christian's obligation and a spiritual gift?

The Bible is clear about what is expected of us as Christians. We are to witness, to have faith, to show hospitality and to support God's work. Like spiritual fruits these things help to define what a Christian is. However, God has given some Christians a particular ability in one or more of these areas. Take evangelism as an example. All of us as Christians are to witness and tell others about God's love for them. Many of us, even without a special gifting in this area, will introduce others to the Christian faith. This is quite different from someone like Billy Graham who has obviously been given the gift of an evangelist. This can be seen from the fact that nearly every time he preaches, thousands become Christians. Yes, we are all commanded to fulfil certain obligations as Christians, but some will be given a special ability to perform a function in a particularly dynamic and supernatural way.

Given by the Holy Spirit

Spiritual gifts are given to believers by the Holy Spirit. It is he who decides what gift each of us receives. Speaking about these gifts, Paul says, *All these are the work of one and the same Spirit, and he gives them to each one, just as he determines* (1 Cor. 12:11). We cannot have a gift just because we want it or even pray for it; it is the Holy Spirit who apportions gifts as he chooses.

The Holy Spirit acts like a manager, providing the people and resources where they are needed. Only he can decide the best strategy for the church. Our job is to ensure that we are exercising our own gifts to the full. Don't feel jealous of the gifts God has given to others in your church, remember that the Holy Spirit knows best who should have what gifts. Neither should you be concerned if some other churches have gifts that don't appear to be present in your own church. In each church there is a reason why certain gifts are present or absent. Rather rejoice in the gifts that your church has been given.

For the Common Good

The Bible tells us the purpose for which gifts are given; they are given *for the common good* (1 Cor. 12:7). Every Christian is given at least one spiritual gift, but spiritual gifts are not given to an individual so that he can boast of his abilities. Neither should anyone selfishly indulge in spiritual experiences which are of no value to the church as a whole. Gifts are given to individuals so that others can benefit.

We are given gifts so that we in turn can give. If a spiritual gift is being used properly, its effect will be seen in the lives of others. The use of our gifts is a act of service to others (1 Pet. 4:10).

No Monopoly
No one person has every spiritual gift (1 Cor. 12:29-30). Some people may have quite a number of different gifts, but no one will be able to claim a monopoly. This is just as well, because it teaches us as Christians to rely on each other. No one person is capable of doing all the work in a church; this would not be desirable anyway, but as we work together, so our pooled resources make effectiveness possible.

Live by Faith
The exercise of these spiritual gifts requires faith. In discussing the use of the gift of prophecy, Paul said that this gift should be exercised *in proportion to our faith*. In other words the gift could be developed more or less strongly in one individual than in another. Paul told Timothy, *Do not neglect your gift* (1 Tim. 4:14) and on another occasion to *fan into flame the gift of God* (2 Tim. 1:6). Through lack of faith or infrequent use it seems that our gift can weaken, therefore vigilance is required on our part.

Gifts and Roles
We can deduce from the passages we have read that people should only do the work within the church that God has equipped them for. I have sat through a number of sermons that were delivered by people

who did not seem to be spiritually gifted for preaching. Though they tried their best, it was to no avail. If they were not equipped to be preachers, they really should not have been doing it. We need to concentrate on the gifts that we have been given and ensure that we are exercising them to the full.

In the New Testament, we find three major lists of spiritual gifts: Romans 12:3-8, 1 Corinthians 12:1-11, 28 and Ephesians 4:11-16. These are not meant to be an exhaustive list of all the spiritual gifts, but do provide us with a good understanding of what kind of things are included under the title of 'spiritual gifts'. It seems that the gifts can be divided into two sections: gifts of speech (e.g. the gift of teaching) and gifts of practical helpfulness (e.g. the gift of serving). Though they function in different ways, all the gifts are equally God-given and are essential for the church.

Space would not permit a detailed description of all the spiritual gifts mentioned in the New Testament; however, some brief comments about those mentioned in the first of the New Testament lists, Romans 12, is appropriate. In this list Paul mentions seven of these gifts: prophecy, serving, teaching, encouraging, contributing, leadership and mercy. He also encourages his readers to use these gifts to the full.

Prophecy
First on the list is the gift of *prophecy*. In the Old Testament there were prophets who declared God's

word to the people. Some of them, like Isaiah, were inspired in a very special way and their words became part of the Bible. This New Testament gift of prophecy is also the ability to declare God's word, but those who exercise it do not fulfil quite the same role as those Old Testament prophets. Once people in the Old Testament were accepted as prophets, their word was not to be questioned. Paul, however, tells us that all prophecies given to the church need to be carefully weighed to see if they are from God. This indicates that they are of a less authoritative nature than the words of the Old Testament prophets.

We need to be careful not to assume that someone who exercises the gift of prophecy must be some kind of spiritual fortune teller. Though some of the Biblical prophets did make predictions about the future, their prophecies dealt mainly with what was happening at the time. They were declaring the word of God to their generation with divine power. I believe this is the sense in which we are to understand the gift of prophecy.

I have sat and listened to many great preachers as they have opened the word of God and expounded it. My understanding of Christianity has increased greatly as a result of the ministry of such men. But there is one preacher I know who seems to be particularly powerful. It is not just that he can explain a passage well, in fact in this regard he is no better than others. But when he preaches, he seems to be able to 'hit the nail on the head' in a remarkable way. He seems aware of what is going on in the lives of his listeners, and is not only sensitive to their needs, but he is able to get right to the bottom of relevant issues through his preaching. He is truly 'inspired', not just giving his hearers something to think about, but powerfully challenging them. In short, he has that prophetic gift which enables him to say the right word at the right time to the right people.

Serving

The next gift that Paul mentions is that of *serving*. The word for serving (diakonia) was originally used of someone who served tables – a waiter. It is the word from which we get the ecclesiastical title of deacon. The person with this gift is someone who is aware of the practical needs within a church and is able to be of help in a gracious way.

I know someone who certainly has this gift. He is a quiet old man who goes to a church where he is hardly noticed, probably because he is not an up-front person. It never ceases to amaze me just how easily he is able to identify people's needs. I could talk to a dozen different people in that church and never notice that there was anything wrong. This old man not only finds out who is in need, but does something about it. Whether it is going to the shops for someone, helping them clean their house or just keeping them company, he does it willingly. People are not embarrassed to ask him for help, they just know he has this special gift. On one occasion I heard that he visited another man who was on his death bed, not just one day, but every day until he died.

What is more, it wasn't just a visit, he also washed, shaved and dressed him each day, with loving devotion. What an important gift serving is!

Teaching
Paul goes on to talk about the gift of *teaching*. The person gifted in this way is able to make the truths of Christianity understandable and bring them to life for others. Teaching does not just involve a repetition of facts, but also applying those truths to the lives of the hearers. The end result of good teaching is that Christians are built up in their faith and strengthened.

In Paul's day there were few Christian books and, with the majority of church members being uneducated, there was an obvious need for teachers. The situation today is different but the need for this gift is just as pressing.

Encouraging
Next Paul mentions the gift of *encouraging*. This gift gives a Christian the ability to strengthen and inspire others to go on and develop in their faith. Many of the Christians in the early church were lower class; some were even slaves. For them daily life was difficult and added to this was the responsibility of a commitment to follow Christ. Being a Christian is wonderful, but it is certainly not an easy life. There has probably been no point in history when being a follower of Jesus Christ has been easy. For Christians, there always have been and always will be discouragements along the way. You have probably been a

113

Christian long enough to realise that sometimes we can feel like giving up.

It is at such times that, we realise what a helpful gift encouragement is. A young man was telling me about his girlfriend. 'She brings out the best in me,' he said. I knew what he meant, for she has the gift of encouragement. She is able to get alongside people who are feeling down and after a while her words of encouragement give them a new lease of life. People feel much better, spiritually lifted and more determined to go on for God after talking to her.

Barnabas was a bit like that. He was nicknamed the 'son of encouragement' (Acts 4:36). Paul, Mark and many others benefited from his ministry. He had the ability to see the potential in someone, even if others could not. Arguably, he could see the potential in others that they could not see in themselves. He would get alongside them to encourage and inspire. Once this was done, Barnabas was happy to sit back and let others take a lead. One can easily imagine the importance of this beautiful gift.

Contributing
Paul then deals with the gift of *contributing to the needs of others*. Bearing in mind the kind of people in the church in his day, it is easy to see how a gift like this would be of great value. The churches of the first century had many poor people as members. Those who had this gift were able to provide for their need. Note that their qualification for this ministry was not wealth, but a spiritual gift. It could well have

been that some of those who gave were poor themselves. We need also to note that all Christians have the duty to support and care for their fellow Christians. These gifted people, however, had a particular ability to identify needs and to give graciously, with utterly pure motives.

Let me stress again that Christians with this gift will not necessarily be wealthy. When I was at Bible College many years ago, I was literally depending on God for my 'daily bread', because I had no visible means of support. Some time ago I was invited to visit a little old Christian lady who was praying for me. When I arrived at her house, I was saddened to see just how poor she was. She lived in one down-stairs room so as to save on heating bills, and had a diet that was absolutely miserable. After assuring me of her constant prayers, she gave me an envelope. In it I found £100. I could have cried, not just because the gift was so generous, but because I knew she really couldn't afford it. She, however, was delighted to give it to me, because she saw this as her ministry. In fact, I later found out that she regularly gave gifts like this to many people. Paul urges those who have the gift of contributing to give generously (Rom. 12:8), this little lady certainly did that.

Leadership

Obviously, if a group of people are to get anywhere they must be led. Leadership is a quality that is found in many non-Christians. Captains of industry, mili-tary generals and politicians could all be described as leaders. But the spiritual gift of leadership goes beyond merely giving orders. Spiritual leadership does not just involve the ability to command respect, but also an attitude of humility, fairness and wisdom.

The person who has the gift of leadership will lead by example. He will not just give orders, but will take the first step himself. He will also be an ideas man. This involves having a vision for the church and the ability to communicate that vision to its members.

Mercy
Finally, Paul talks about those who have the gift of *mercy*. Generally speaking, those who need mercy are people who are in some sort of difficulty. This difficulty may involve sickness, suffering or even some emotional problem. Paul says that mercy should be shown cheerfully. In other words, a person with this gift will offer comfort to the hurting, not out of duty, but joyfully.

There is nothing worse when I am upset or ill than to have someone visit me who spends the whole time moaning and complaining. Frankly, I would rather be alone. But I know of some people who have such a cheerful disposition that they make me feel better. Even if I am really down they can empathise to the point that I feel they really understand. This is the gift of mercy. It is much more than just pity. It is the ability to make a real difference to someone's life when they are at their lowest.

These are just some of the spiritual gifts mentioned in the New Testament. As I have already stated, there are other lists to be found. Remember that these gifts are not given to Christians for their own benefit, but so that they can benefit others. If we keep this priority in mind, then we will be truly useful to the church.

What are my Gifts?

You might be thinking, 'How do I know what gifts I have, and how do I develop my gifts once I find them?' The first step is to pray. This may sound obvious, but it is vital. God is the one who gives spiritual gifts, so you need to be in touch with him. As you pray, read what the Bible has to say on the subject. Study and familiarise yourself with what is involved in exercising the spiritual gifts.

There also needs to be a daily submission to God's will. Gifts are given for a purpose. God has a plan for each church and he gives gifts accordingly. You need to be open to his will, whatever that may be. God will then use your willingness as he equips you for service.

It would be good to examine your aspirations for Christian service. By that I mean, what contribution would you like to make towards God's work? What do you feel drawn to? Some people think that God's will for their lives will be unpleasant. They obviously do not understand who God is. I for one get great pleasure from exercising my gifts. God wants us to feel fulfilled in serving him. If you have any desires for a certain kind of work within your church, that may be an indication that your gifts lie in that direction. On the other hand if you dread having to do some of the things you see other people in your church doing, this too could be an indication that God has a different kind of work for you to do.

Why not ask a mature Christian who knows you well to help you discover your gifts? I am sure they will be delighted and will be able to give a more objective assessment. If they can see results from some aspect of your Christian service, then you can be fairly sure that you have a gift in that area.

This of course pre-supposes that you are actively involved in your church. There is no point in trying to identify some gift if you are sitting about doing nothing. Only when you get involved in the activities of your church can you discover what potential you have.

Once you discover your gifts, you then need to exercise them, in order that they may develop. Paul instructed Timothy to *fan into flame the gift of God* (2 Tim. 1:6). Practice makes perfect, and to an extent this is true of spiritual gifts.

A young friend of mine was only sixteen years old when he preached his first sermon. The night before he hardly slept because he was so nervous about it. Such was his fear that he wrote his message out word for word and memorized it. He practised preaching to himself several times in front of a mirror and timed himself. He planned to preach for twenty-five minutes. When the time came for him to stand up in front of the congregation, he was so terrified that he literally shook. The message itself lasted about ten minutes as he mumbled his way through, skipping many important bits. It is not that he didn't have the gift of preaching. Time has shown that he does. He simply had little practice. It is important to be patient with yourself as you polish up the gifts God has given you.

Discovering your gifts and practising them is easier in some churches than in others. If you come from a small but active church, you may find that people encourage you to be involved and to practise your gifts, but if your church is large and the activities are dominated by a few key people, then it may be very different. Don't be discouraged. Try to get as involved as you can. Just remember that God has given gifts to your church, and some of those gifts are being given via you. Persevere, and you will discover many opportunities for service.

PRAYER:
Father, Thank you for the spiritual gifts you have given me. Thank you that you want to use me in your service, to build your church and demonstrate your love and power.

Help me to use these gifts wisely, so that I can help others and glorify you. I ask for the opportunity to be of service. Amen.

Chapter 10

Remembering

For the Jews of the Old Testament, ritual and ceremony were important. The same is true for Christians. There are two ceremonies in particular that are important, those of Baptism and Communion. In this chapter we will think of both of these in turn.

Baptism
What is baptism? The Greek word *baptizo* means 'to plunge, dip or immerse' something in water. That is exactly what is done in a baptism; the person who is being baptized is immersed in water and then brought back up again. Though this may seem a rather strange ritual, it has powerful symbolic significance which we will examine later on. The question is, why are people baptised? Why is this ceremony necessary?

The answer is simple: baptism is necessary because Jesus commanded it. In the great commission (Matt. 28:19) Jesus gave instructions to his disciples, not just to witness to other people, but also to baptise their converts. This baptism was to be a symbol of their commitment to Christ. Later on in Acts 2:41 we read that *those who accepted his message were baptised*. Clearly the lesson had been learnt and the ceremony of baptism was very much part of Christian practice from the beginning.

Statement of Faith

Baptism is a *statement of faith*. It is a sign of commitment to Christ. Baptism in itself does not save anyone or make him a Christian, but it is a public confession of the fact that someone has trusted in Jesus Christ as Saviour.

Baptism is like a wedding ring. When I married, my wife and I exchanged rings. Those rings were a symbol of our marriage. The rings did not make us man and wife; it was our vows and commitment to each other that did that, but the rings are a visible symbol of our marriage relationship. In much the same way, baptism is a means by which Christians declare publicly that they belong to Jesus Christ.

If my wife and I had decided not to exchange rings we would still have loved each other as much. The rings were and are a symbol of a relationship that already exists between us, an evidence that we belong to each other. A reminder to us, but also a sign to others that we are married. In much the same way baptism is a sign to the world that we belong to Jesus.

Statement of Devotion

Secondly, baptism is a *statement of devotion*. It was the custom in the Roman world, for a soldier to swear an oath of allegiance to the Emperor. This oath was known as a sacramentum (from which we get the word 'sacrament'). The soldier was making a vow to obey his Emperor and serve him loyally. In baptism we declare our devotion to Christ and commit ourselves to his service. Paul urged the Christians at Rome to lay their lives on the line for Christ (Rom. 12:1), and follow him with unswerving devotion. As a person is baptised he is publicly stating that his allegiance is to Jesus Christ. He will follow every command as a soldier follows the command of his senior officer, even if such obedience costs everything.

Statement of Change

But baptism is more than just a statement of faith and devotion, it is also a *statement of change*. In Galatians 3:27 Paul states: *for all of you were baptised into Christ and have clothed yourselves with Christ*. In this verse we are presented with the imagery of someone taking off their dirty old clothes and putting on new ones.

Once a tramp came to our door asking for some food. His clothes looked so tattered that I gave him a nice suit that I rarely wore. The next day he came back, not to ask for more food, but to show me the suit that he was now wearing. I remember commenting that he looked like a new man.

In a very real sense we as Christians have been given new spiritual clothing. We have removed the filthy clothes of sin and they have been replaced with clothes of righteousness, made for us through Christ's sacrifice. We were sinful, but now we are holy in God's sight. Baptism symbolises this marvellous transformation.

Statement of Identification

Baptism is also a *statement of identification*. Through baptism, we identify with Christ in the three acts that underwrite our salvation, namely his death, burial and resurrection. In Colossians 2:12 Paul writes about our *having been buried with him in baptism and raised with him through your faith in the power of God who raised him from the dead*.

In baptism, a person is lowered into the water. Symbolically he is dead. Just as Jesus died on the cross to destroy the power of sin, so we are to die to sin in our lives. The past is to be put behind, we are no longer to be slaves to sin, but are to turn our backs on all wrongdoing.

In Romans 6:11 Paul said to *count yourselves dead to sin*. There is no point in trying to lead a dead man astray or to entice him into sinning. He is dead and therefore will never respond. In the same way, we as Christians are to be so absorbed with Jesus Christ, that sin has no hold on us.

After death comes burial. In baptism, when someone is submerged under the water, he is symbolising the burial of Christ. Paul said, *We were therefore buried with him through baptism into death* (Rom. 6:4). In this sense our baptism is a funeral. We are saying farewell to our old sinful life. We want nothing more to do with it. It is a thing of the past and must not be allowed to return. We have finished with it forever, so we bury out of sight.

Of course the person who is being baptised is not left submerged under the water, but is lifted out again. This symbolises Christ's resurrection from the dead. Paul tells us that *we were therefore buried with him through baptism into death in order that, just as*

Christ was raised from the dead through the glory of the Father, we too may live a new life (Rom. 6:4).

Just as God raised Jesus from the dead, he wants us to live a new life – one in which we say 'no' to sin, and in which we seek to obey his commands, and reflect his very character in everything we say and do.

Statement of Unity

Finally, baptism is a *statement of unity* with the body of Christ, the church. Whatever our background, all Christians are part of the same body (1 Cor. 12:13). We belong to each other and are united not just by blood ties, but by the Holy Spirit. We are one because through his death, Jesus has made us children of God. By being baptized we acknowledge the bond we share within the church.

Bearing in mind all that we have read, it is obvious that baptism is a serious matter and not something that can be entered into lightly. It is however a command of Christ and therefore something that all Christians should obey. The New Testament does not envisage the possibility of an unbaptised Christian. I know of instances where people were Christians for many years before they were baptised. This should not be the case. If you are a Christian and have committed your life to Christ, then you should publicly demonstrate that commitment by being baptised.*

---

* Some Christians practise infant baptism, whereby they baptize the children of Christian parents. I do not personally endorse this view, but I recognise and respect the genuineness of those who do.

Communion

The other ceremony that is important to Christians is Communion (sometimes called the Lord's Supper). Again to the onlooker this might seem a strange ritual – a plate of bread and a cup of wine being passed from one to another with each eating and drinking. What can we discover about the origins of this ceremony and what is its significance?

Luke gives us a description of the events of the Last Supper Jesus shared with his disciples (Luke 22:15-20). We are told that this meal took place during the Passover. For Jews the Passover celebration was a very significant event as it was a celebration of their deliverance from slavery in Egypt and the establishment of a new relationship (or covenant) with God. During this meal Jesus talked about a new relationship with God which would be established as a result of his sacrifice.

The Saviour took bread and wine. The bread was to represent his body and the wine his blood. He broke the loaf of bread and said to his disciples, *This is my body given for you; do this in remembrance of me* (v. 19). Each of them took a piece and ate it. He picked up the cup of wine and said, *This cup is the new covenant in my blood, which is poured out for you* (v. 20). They all took a sip from the cup. Just a simple act, yet Jesus asked his followers to repeat this ceremony and in doing so to remember him.

What does it all mean?

Reflection

When Jesus shared the Last Supper with his disciples, he was thinking about his death and the salvation that it would bring to his followers. In the Communion service, therefore, we reflect on the death of Jesus. Of course, the bread and wine are symbols, it is not that Jesus is literally being sacrificed again. But as we re-enact this event, the significance of his death is brought freshly before us.

If Jesus had not gone to the cross, we would still be condemned sinners with no hope of a reprieve. We do not merit salvation and would consequently be under God's judgment. While hanging on the cross Jesus took the punishment for our sins as if they were his own (1 Pet. 2:24). He removed the barrier of sin which keeps us from God and made possible a new relationship between us and God.

By taking the bread and drinking from the cup we are recognising the significance of the cross, and expressing the belief that salvation comes as a result of Christ's death. Just as baptism is an outward expression of our commitment to Christ, so participating in Communion is an expression of our faith in Christ and his work on the cross.

Although the Communion service is a memorial, it should also be a joyful occasion. Jesus died, but he rose from the dead and is alive. Every time we remember him in this way, we need to bear in mind that he is with us spiritually and can appreciate our worship. Specifically Jesus said, *do this in remembrance of me* (Luke 22:19). Those disciples, having lived with Jesus for three years, would have had many lovely memories to cherish. They would have thought about his love for children, his healing power, his wisdom and integrity. These thoughts would come naturally to them as they broke the bread and reflected on the life of their master. Jesus was dead, yes! But now he is alive and we are welcomed to share this time with him.

Hope

The Communion service is not just about the past, or even the present, it is also about the future. Before Jesus broke the bread he said, *I will not eat it again until it finds fulfilment in the kingdom of God* (v. 16). As we participate in the Communion service we are looking forward to another celebration at which Jesus will be the host. That will be a celebration laid on for us in heaven. At the Communion we celebrate our salvation, but on that day we will experienced salvation in all its fullness.

As Christians we are 'saved' and possess eternal life. However, we still have to live in a fallen world where there is suffering and pain. We also continue to sin, unwillingly though it may be. By faith we can appreciate what our salvation involves, but we will not experience salvation to the full until we get to Heaven. Meanwhile, as we take the bread and the cup, we look forward to that great event.

Declaration

It could also be said that Communion is a declaration or a proclaiming to the world that salvation is available (1 Cor. 11:26). The very centre of the Christian message is the death of Christ. As we break bread and drink from the cup we are showing others how salvation can be attained. We are declaring that Christ is the way to forgiveness and a relationship with God.

How should we Celebrate?

Having thought about the meaning of Communion, it is important to go on and ask how it should be celebrated. The Bible does not give us exact details of how or when Communion services were conducted in the early church, but there are some clues for us here and there. In Acts 2:42-46, for example, we are told that the Christians used the intimate surroundings of a home in which to celebrate Communion. These times together were characterised by joy and a deep sense of reverence. Then, in Acts 20:7 we read that Communion was celebrated on the first day of the week, Sunday. The impression we are given is that of a weekly event. However, we must not assume that Communion was only practised on Sundays. In 1 Corinthians 11:26 Paul wrote, *whenever you eat this bread*, inferring that this ceremony could be conducted at any time.

There seems to have been some variety to this celebration. Some members of the congregation would offer prayers, others would give some teaching and there would be hymn singing (1 Cor. 14:26). The emphasis seems to be on spontaneity rather than a highly organised programme. It was also an event that people could participate in. There is no evidence to suggest that Communion should only be conducted by members of an ordained ministry.

With this limited information, it would be hard to develop too regimented an order of service for the celebration of Communion. There would appear to be a fair amount of freedom for individual expression. Two churches could have a very different type of service and yet each could justifiably claim that theirs was a 'Biblical pattern of worship'. We must steer clear of dogmatism and the criticism of other churches who celebrate it in a different way. However, we can lay down some general principles.

Firstly, Communion should be celebrated regularly. We might even want to say that it should be celebrated weekly, and there is biblical precedent for that view. Secondly, the essential simplicity of the occasion should be kept in mind; it is designed for specifically remembering Christ and all that he did. Thirdly, it is a celebration for all the followers of Jesus and none should be excluded. Christ himself is the host of this celebration as he was during the Last Supper, and he welcomes all true Christians to remember him. Some churches allow only Christians from their own denomination to celebrate Communion with them. This exclusive practice is unbiblical and undermines what is intended to be a beautiful celebration for all of God's family.

Right Attitude

There is a warning given to all who celebrate Communion. Paul tells us, *Therefore, whoever eats the bread and drinks the cup of the Lord in an unworthy manner will be guilty of sinning against the body and blood of the Lord* (1 Cor. 11:27). Clearly, we need to be careful about our attitude when we participate in Communion. But what does it mean to sin against the body and blood of Jesus Christ?

To put it simply, we would be sinning against Christ if we did not recognise the importance of Communion while we were participating in it. This attitude of complacency could manifest itself in a whole variety of ways. For example, it would be possible for a Christian to take part in a Communion service just because he is in the habit of doing so. It can become a bit of a ritual because we celebrate it so regularly.

There have been times when I have sat in a Communion service but my mind has been miles away. While people have been pouring out their hearts to God in worship, my thoughts have been on the football match I saw the previous night. I have sung the hymns, but without even thinking about the words. I have been there in body, but not in spirit. I have been going through the motions, but my heart was elsewhere. At times I have even prayed without really meaning the words I was saying.

Impressing the person who sits beside me in church is easy enough, but it is impossible to deceive God. God is not impressed by my mere attendance at a church meeting; he scrutinises my heart and accurately reads the level of my sincerity and involvement.

Another sin we can commit at the Communion service is that of harbouring unconfessed sin in our lives. Some people think that God turns a blind eye to the way they live, provided they go to church on Sunday. This is not the case. God is just as concerned at the way we are living the rest of the week. If I have not been honouring Christ by my lifestyle from Monday to Saturday, any words of worship I offer on Sunday are pretty cheap. Our celebration of Communion should be the culmination of a week in which we have dedicated our lives to God. Our celebration of Communion is not just a religious event we take part in one day each week, it is part of an every-day commitment to Christ. Only when we truly live for Christ every day can we really appreciate the significance of Communion. Likewise, in celebrating Communion we are drawn closer to Christ and that enhances our relationship with him.

PRAYER:
Father, thank you for the death and resurrection of your Son Jesus Christ and for the life he has given me.

Help me to be obedient to him through baptism and glorify him in the celebration of Communion. Amen.

Chapter 11

Living in a Material World

Each generation of Christians will have their own problems to deal with. Throughout church history there have been theological controversies, denominational divisions, as well as times of real spiritual coldness. Christians have found themselves not just battling with the world and the Devil, but also among themselves and with their own personal apathy. During such times, many have found the need to reassess their priorities and get back to an intimate relationship with God.

It is my conviction that one of the biggest threats which Christians in the West are facing today is that of materialism. I am not exaggerating when I say that many churches have ground to a halt and become ineffective because their members have become more committed to commercial success than to Christ. As this is a book for young Christians I think it is necessary to mention this most dangerous of threats.

In 1 Timothy 6:8, 9 Paul writes, *But if we have food and clothing, we will be content with that. People who want to get rich fall into temptation and a trap and into many foolish and harmful desires that plunge men into ruin and destruction.* Clearly Paul saw the dangers of materialism even in his day.

Which God

When someone becomes a Christian they not only accept Jesus as Saviour, but as Lord also. The fact that Jesus is Lord of my life means that all that I am and have belongs to him. This includes my wallet! Everything that I earn is his and I am a mere steward of these possessions. This way of thinking is of course alien to our society, for it worships the god of money. Society values people by what they have rather than what they are. Jesus stated quite clearly that we need to make a choice either to follow the true God or the god of materialism (Luke 16:13).

The problem is that many Christians have become like the society around them. They are happy for God to rule their lives provided they can cling to all their possessions at the same time. Some Christians have even developed a strand of teaching, claiming that material possessions are a sign of God's blessing on their lives. This is no more than an excuse for an excessive lifestyle. Jesus himself chose to lay aside the grandeur of heaven and be born in a cattle shed. He calls us to follow his example in rejecting our materialistic culture.

It strikes me that some of the most outstanding Christians and vibrant churches in the world are found in deprived countries where there is little by way of material possessions. For the Christians of Ethiopia or China who have so few possessions, Christ really is Lord, for they surrender what they have, however little, to God's service and as a result experience God's work in their lives in an extraordinary way. If riches are a sign of blessing, then why are so many churches in the third world growing so fast while many churches in Britain are in decline?

Money of course is a necessity and not evil in itself. However, the accumulation of wealth should not be life's objective. Money can be dangerous because it can dominate our lives, leading us away from God. As the writer of Proverbs wisely said: *Give me neither poverty nor riches, but give me only my daily bread. Otherwise, I may have too much and disown you and say, 'Who is the LORD?' Or I may become poor and steal, and so dishonour the name of my God* (Prov. 30:8-9).

It would of course be both wrong and foolish of me to try and legislate for anyone else as to how they should live. Blanket rules governing how Christians spend their money are of little value, but I want to mention three considerations that should influence us and make us think.

Self Sacrifice

First of all, it should be mentioned that self-sacrifice is an integral part of the Christian life. In chapter 1 we thought about the words of Jesus in Luke 9:23 when he said that all those who wanted to follow him must take up their cross and deny themselves. Crucifixion was a brutally effective form of capital punishment. Dying to ourselves and to our own rights affects every part of our lives. We can no longer claim to possess anything for we are to think of ourselves as dead, only Christ lives in us. Our exclusive purpose in life is to serve and please him. This is what Paul meant when he said in Galatians 2:20: *I have been crucified with Christ and I no longer live, but Christ lives in me. The life I live in the body, I live by faith in the Son of God, who loved me and gave himself for me.*

Christianity should not be some morbid plunge into asceticism. Jesus does not expect us to dress in potato sacks and eat cold porridge every day. In the very next verse Jesus said that if we lose our lives for his sake, we would actually save them. There is little value in deliberately hurting ourselves in order to gain merit. There are no brownie points for masochism. We do, however, need to free ourselves from the tyranny of selfishness if we are to serve Christ with single-minded devotion, and this will inevitably involve disciplined self-sacrifice. Our lifestyles must reflect the fact that our ambitions and desires are put to one side so that his wishes can govern our actions.

There is little point in claiming total allegiance to Christ if his will is not sought in the buying of a new car, house or clothes. We cannot say that he is Lord of our lives if we manage our wages without any thought as to what he might want us to do with our money. All too often we satisfy all our desires and then give to God whatever is left. The opposite should be the case. We should take what we need to be comfortable and give the rest to God. This should be the material consequence of a life that has been truly 'crucified'.

Real Need

Secondly, we need to consider the very real needs that exist in our world. While he was here on earth, Jesus demonstrated his concern for the poor, the hungry and the oppressed. As his followers we continue his work. We are the body of Christ and need to do whatever he would do if he were in our shoes today.

Jesus cared deeply for the needy people of his day, and cares for the needy today also. He is concerned for the homeless and the unemployed. He cares for the AIDS victims of Zambia and the inhabitants of 'Smoky Mountain', a rubbish tip outside Manila that hundreds call home. His concern is vast enough to reach out to the one billion people who go to bed hungry each night.

We too need to share this concern. Our lifestyle must reflect a compassion for the 40,000 children under the age of five who die daily of malnutrition, for the world's 18,000,000 refugees, for the 200 million children who have no access to clean water, or the 150 million who languish in child labour. Only when we show this kind of compassion can we claim to be following Christ.

Being realistic, we will never be able to solve the problem of poverty in the world, but that is not an excuse for doing nothing. We must show compassion and live in such a way as to be able to make a difference in some lives, if not all. God does not judge us for what we cannot do, but for what we can do, and don't.

Investing

The third consideration we need to bear in mind, is the positive investment for God that we will be able to make if we are careful about how we live. Jesus said to his followers, *Do not store up for yourselves treasures on earth* (Matt. 6:19). They were to invest in something more valuable and lasting than material possessions. Their investment would be in God's kingdom. One Christian writer has put it this way:

> To transpose the recommendation to the twentieth century, if televisions can go on the blink, cars depreciate, fashionable clothes go out of date, if bonds and jewels can be stolen, insurance companies go bankrupt, banks fail, and war and inflation destroy property and the value of money, it would make more sense to devote our energies to accumulating a celestial fortune.[1]

God gave his only Son because he wanted to invest in our lives and bring us into his kingdom. What kind of investments are we prepared to make to see this kingdom extended?

For some Christians giving has been at the level of a gratuity. They will give to God only the small change that they find in their pockets. For others it is an emotional sacrifice. In other words, 'I will give when I feel like it.' For others still, there is a good intention in their giving that says 'I'll give more when I have got it, provided it does not interfere with my lifestyle'. However, if we are to genuinely sacrifice, if we really care about the poor, if we want to make a significant heavenly investment, then we need to give as generously and willingly as possible.

A Disciplined Lifestyle

Assuming that we want to live by these three principles, how do we decide what is a need and what is simply a want? Again I cannot lay down blanket laws to answer this question, because my needs may well be very different from yours. However, I would like to mention an eight point plan which I have found of great help in my life. This plan (adapted from the book *A Celebration of Discipline*[2]) has helped me decide what I should spend, and has proved a useful guide to my lifestyle. You may find it to be a useful guide for you also!

1. Learn to buy things for their usefulness not their status. Brand name clothes, for example, are often much more expensive than equally good non-brand names.

2. Avoid situations where the urge to spend money may be overwhelming. If you can't walk into a clothes shop without buying something, then avoid the temptation alltogether.

3. Learn to give things away. This is difficult at first, especially if you like the things you are giving, but it will become a habit. Why should you have several coats when someone you know does not even have one?

4. Don't be taken in by gadgets. Do you really need a watch that gives you twelve time zones and is waterproof to a depth of ten metres.

5. Be cautious about catalogues and 'buy now pay later' schemes. They only encourage you to buy what you don't need.

6. Imagine how a full-time worker or missionary lives and try to emulate their lifestyle.

7. Learn to question the validity of any non-essential purchase. If, for example, I buy a CD, I need to bear in mind that the £13.50 it costs me could feed one Rwandan child for five weeks, or provide 8,000 aspirins for medical work in Angola, or print 11 Russian Bibles. This does not make the purchase wrong, but it should make me think about priorities.

8. Avoid everything that may distract you from your main goal in life, the kingdom of God.

How Do I Give

The next question is an obvious one. How should I give my money? Let me suggest that there are two ways of giving. You can give as you see needs arise. The Bible teaches that those who have what they need and more, should give what they can to those who have not (Luke 3:11). I have sometimes come across needy people whom I was able to help there and then.

This has included missionaries and full-time Christian workers who rely on the generosity of other Christians for their support.

Another way of giving is through the church. My own church, for example, is involved in supporting various Christian ministries around the world as well as financing Christian activity in our own area. Each week we have an offering and our combined giving is then allocated by the leaders of the church to where they think it is most needed.

It is important that our giving is systematic. No matter how much or how little you earn, you are probably in a position to give something each week. Paul instructed the Christians in Corinth, *On the first day of every week, each of you should set aside a sum of money in keeping with his income* (1 Cor. 16:2). Clearly systematic giving is not just a good idea, it is also a Biblical principal.

Jesus clearly taught that it was not the amount that we give that counts, but the sacrifice we make. On one occasion he was at the temple and watched as people came along to give their offering (Mark 12:41-44). Many rich people were putting in large amounts of money, but this did not impress Jesus, for he knew that they had plenty left over for themselves. Then a poor widow approached. She put in only two very small copper coins worth only pennies. Calling his disciples over to him he said, *This poor widow has put more into the treasury than all the others* (v. 43). The reason, simply because she had little, if anything, left after her giving, whereas the others had plenty. God was pleased with her sacrifice and unimpressed with the comparatively small sacrifice of the people who could afford to give more.

It is not so much what we give that counts, but that we give what we can. If we cultivate the habit of giving regularly and sacrificially, then we will have learnt to please God as the poor widow in Jesus' story did.

Of course there is no point in giving to others and to God if we are going to be miserable about it. Our attitude in giving is of great importance. In 2 Corinthians 9:7 we are told that *God loves a cheerful giver*. It is true that as we give, we are doing without. However, others are being blessed and we should rejoice in the pleasure they get in receiving from us. This should inspire us to a willingness that delights in self-sacrifice.

Blessings of Giving

When we give there is a great deal to be delighted about. Firstly, as we learn to give willingly, so we discover that material possessions become less important to us. The simplicity of a sacrificial life allows us to have a deeper fellowship with God. I have often noted that some of the most godly people I know are people who give generously.

Secondly, as we give to the poor, the needy and the hurting, so we demonstrate the love of Christ. This love flows through us to the people to whom we are giving. In this way we identify with Christ and experience the joy of true love.

Thirdly, in giving, we can contribute to the kingdom of God. It is impossible for me to be working in a missionary school in Zambia, a mission clinic in India, or with an evangelist in the slums of Brazil, all at the same time. Indeed I may never visit any of these places. But I can give! My money can contribute to the work in these and many more places, provided I really want to invest in the Kingdom of God. Whether I can give a lot or even a small amount, all that I can give will be an investment for heaven.

PRAYER:
Father, thank you that you gave your Son so that I could have life. Thank you also for the good things you give me every day and for providing me with food and clothing and a place to live. I recognise that all good things come from you.

Help me not to be selfish in my lifestyle, rather help me to be generous and wise in the use of my resources. Protect me from the love of material possessions and help me to live the kind of lifestyle that reflects my devotion to you. Amen.

References
1. John White, *Money Isn't God*, p. 148.
2. Richard Foster, *A Celebration of Discipline*, pp. 78-82.

Chapter 12

Pass it On

I have always believed that good news should be shared and this is especially true of the good news (gospel) of salvation. As Christians we have something that is infinitely more valuable than anything this world has to offer, namely eternal life. We have been given this life because of our relationship with Jesus Christ. It is important to know, however, that we are not the only people Jesus loves or died for. Jesus also wants to give life to your family, friends and workmates who are not Christians. It is your job to tell them about him.

Telling Others
Time and time again in the New Testament, we are encouraged and even commanded to share our faith with others. Think about the words of Jesus to his disciples in Matthew 28:18-20:

All authority in heaven and on earth has been given to me. Therefore go and make disciples of all nations, baptizing them in the name of the Father and the Son and of the Holy Spirit, and teaching them to obey everything I have commanded you.

As far as I am aware this is the only time that Jesus stated that he had all authority in heaven and on earth. It is no coincidence, then, that he made this statement just before giving his disciples this great commission to witness to others. With all the authority of heaven and earth he commanded them, and commands us, to take this great message of hope to a dying world.

This is a tremendous command. Take Christianity to all nations! Needless to say, no one person could do this, but each of us must play our part in making this possible. This responsibility rests squarely on the shoulders of every true Christian. On another occasion Jesus said that the proof of our love for him would be demonstrated by our obedience to his commands (John 14:15). If we do love him, then that love will inspire us to obey his command by telling others about him. Conversely, if you are not actively sharing your faith with others, then your love for Jesus must be brought into question.

Think of all the people you know who are not Christians. You work with some of them, or go to school with them. Some of your neighbours are not Christians, maybe even some of your family members. You have a unique opportunity to witness to these people because you already have a relationship with them. You are better placed than anyone to reach them for Christ.

Christians in the early church took this command to heart. When the Holy Spirit came upon them at Pentecost, the first thing they did was to witness (Acts 2). They continued doing this, talking to everyone they met until that tiny community of Christians had grown to thousands. A little later on a great persecution broke out in Jerusalem so the Christians had to flee for their lives (Acts 8:1-4). Even on the run they were witnessing, gossiping the gospel to anyone who was prepared to listen. The result was that people all over the Roman empire became Christians.

Ambassadors

In 2 Corinthians 5:20 Paul states, *We are therefore Christ's ambassadors, as though God were making his appeal through us.* This is quite a statement bearing in mind what an ambassador is. According to my dictionary, there are two definitions of an ambassador: (1) diplomatic official of the highest rank, appointed and accredited as representative; (2) one who stands for, represents and actively propagates a particular belief, set of values or culture.

God has launched a great plan to save the world from sin. Through Jesus he has opened channels of communication with mankind and he wants to establish a peace treaty with all who are willing to begin a relationship with him. In this great task, you and I are God's ambassadors. We are the highest ranking diplomats that God has and he wants us to represent him and his kingdom to the world. What a great privilege!

I have often wondered why God did not use the mighty angels to be his ambassadors. Surely they could do a better job than me. Whatever the reason, we need to understand that being God's mouthpiece is such a privilege, it is inconceivable that any

Christian should refuse to play their part in telling others about the love of God.

Witnesses
You will be my witnesses, said Jesus, *in Jerusalem, and in all Judea and Samaria, and to the ends of the earth* (Acts 1:8). The Christians who first received this message were already in Jerusalem. What Jesus was saying to them is that they needed to start where they were, to make sure that everyone around them had the opportunity of responding to their message. Then they were to reach out even farther to other areas and countries. They were to take the message to the farthest parts of the world. This job will never be finished until everyone, everywhere, has the opportunity of responding to God.

All of us need to be witnessing to our natural peer groups and to those people we come into contact with in everyday life. Then we need to reach out to people in our area that are outside of our natural peer group and that we would never normally meet. The ethnic minorities, street people, young children, the elderly, the youths who hang about our streets. We may never come across them in the normal course of events, but they need to hear and so we should be prepared to go out of our way, to feel uncomfortable, so that we can tell them about Christ.

What about other countries? It seems to me that each local church, if it is really to be obedient to Christ's command, should have a concern for un-reached people wherever they are. Not every member of your church will become a missionary and go to a foreign country, but every member should be praying for other countries and giving to missionaries who work there. It may well be that someone within your church feels called to serve God abroad. That person might even be you. If so then the church must fully identify with their work, and play a full supporting role from home.

There is so much to do, both in this country and elsewhere. So many people do not know God and are living lives that are enslaved to sin. We have a message that can free them and give them life. I cannot emphasize how vital it is that we share our faith with as many people as possible.

In recent years there has been a lot of talk about AIDS. This deadly virus has claimed many lives in Britain alone. Supposing another virus were to strike, one that was much more deadly and contagious than AIDS. Imagine that thousands every day were dying and that you had the only known antidote in your bathroom cupboard. What would you do? Obviously you would share your antidote with everyone you came across. It would be wicked not to do so.

Sin is the most deadly virus the world has ever known. Everyone is dying from it. It really is terrible that so many Christians are not sharing the antidote of Christ's forgiveness with others. The responsibility is ours, we must not fail!

Assuming that we do want to be active in evangelism, how can we learn to be effective? It seems to me that there are four requirements which must be met before effectiveness is possible.

Knowing Christ

Firstly, we need to have a vibrant, life-changing relationship with Jesus Christ. Witnessing, after all, is not just about what we say, but the kind of people we are. You could eloquently explain what Christianity is to someone, but if your lifestyle does not prove that Christianity actually works, then they are not likely to believe you. In any case it would be hypocrisy for you to urge someone to give their life to Christ if you are not submitting yours.

Paul made this bold statement to the Corinthians, *Therefore I urge you to imitate me* (1 Cor. 4:16). Later in the same letter he qualified it by saying, *Follow my example, as I follow the example of Christ* (1 Cor. 11:1). Clearly Paul lived a life that was worthy of imitation. He made the point that his life was so modelled on Christ, that if these young Christians followed his example, they would indirectly be following Christ. This is the kind of life we need to live if we are to be successful in evangelism.

I have witnessed to many people who have really struggled to grasp what Christianity is all about. However much I tell them about God's love and the life-changing power that he can give, the penny just does not drop. These are spiritual matters and are therefore difficult to comprehend. My life, however, speaks volumes. Although my friends don't understand what Christianity is, they can see what it does in my life. The way I live can provide tangible evidence that what I say is true. The closer I am in my relationship with Christ, the greater this evidence will be. Consequently my witness will be more effective.

It has been my experience that the lives of other Christians have made a greater impact on me than what they said. As a result of seeing how Christians live, the holiness and joy they radiated, I gave my own life to Jesus. A Christian's lifestyle will say more than a thousand words.

Knowing the Bible

A second requirement if we are to be effective in evangelism is a detailed knowledge of the word of God. Through the Bible God reveals himself; his love, justice, wisdom and many other aspects of his character. How will we be able to explain to our non-Christian friends who God is if we have not become familiar with the Bible. It is imperative that we get to grips with it and acquire at least a working knowledge of its contents.

Some years ago, doing some door to door work in my neighbourhood. I went to one house and discovered that the owner, a well educated business-man, was particularly interested in religion. We talked together for well over an hour, discussing different ideas and thoughts. Though he believed the Bible was true, he had some very wrong ideas about who God was and what was involved in salvation. I don't know where these ideas came from, but they were certainly not Biblical.

Remembering some of the things I had been taught in church, I began correcting him. 'But the Bible says something very different from that,' I insisted, at which point he replied, 'Show me where.' I was so embarrassed. Although I knew he was wrong, my knowledge of the Bible was so lacking that I could not prove it. There was nothing I could do. I had lost all credibility. That day I learned a very important lesson. Don't shoot your mouth off about anything unless you can show from the Bible that what you are saying is true.

Learning to use the Bible effectively is one of the keys to successfully sharing our faith. It is the living word of God which is sharper than a two-edged sword (Heb. 4:12). It can cut through the hypocrisy and deception of any idea or belief and pierce the very heart of our listeners. I am always interested to hear Billy Graham preaching. He frequently and skilfully quotes Bible verses during his message. I am convinced that this is a major reason for his success as an evangelist.

Discovering Prayer
Thirdly, in order to be effective in our evangelism, we need to discover the power of prayer. However eloquent we might be in our presentation of the Christian message, however convincing in our arguments, however sincere and passionate in our presentation of truth, we are utterly unable to awaken anyone to their spiritual need. This is the work of the Holy Spirit and we must learn to pray that his power will be at work as we witness.

Historians have shown that some of the great revivals of history were started in prayer meetings.

Christians began to realise that they needed God's power if they were to reach their own generation. They tapped into this power through prayer and were amazed by what followed.

Once, during a lecture on evangelism, I asked a group of students what in their opinion was the key to successful evangelism. Was it powerful preaching, the use of good literature, or perhaps the training of church members? One of the students, a Korean, began to talk about his church, only ten years in existence yet already with a congregation of three thousand. He was convinced the key was their emphasis on prayer. Every morning hundreds of church members would get together to pray before going off to their work. This prayer-saturated church not only expected people in their town to become Christians, they also proved their point by seeing their church membership growing year after year.

Prayer is that vital component. As we pray specifically for those to whom we have witnessed, the Holy Spirit begins to work in their lives, convicting them of their sin and drawing them towards repentance. Only the Holy Spirit can bring a person to faith in Jesus Christ. Through prayer we can implore the Holy Spirit to do his work.

Learning Compassion

The fourth condition to effective evangelism is to have a Christ-like compassion. Evangelism is hard work and there are many knocks along the way. You will have found that some of your friends do not want to know about your faith. They like you, but they are just not interested in what you have to say about Christianity. It would be wrong to ram it down their throats, or to be tactless in presenting them with the claims of Christianity, but at the same time they need to know the spiritual danger they are in. You would not be a true friend if you did not warn them. This is a difficult tightrope to walk. All too often, Christians decide not to bother witnessing to their friends, it is simply too inconvenient.

If witnessing to friends is hard, then reaching out to comparative strangers is even more difficult. I come across many people whom I don't know well, but have some kind of contact with. Some of them are neighbours, some are people I meet in the bus on the way to work, many are just casual acquaintances of one sort or another. One thing I can be sure of, they all need a relationship with Jesus Christ. But finding the opportunity to talk to them is difficult. It may mean going out of my way to try and initiate some kind of conversation.

Whether we are witnessing to friends or to people we only know vaguely, there is always the possibility that we might offend, or be ridiculed. These opportunities to witness do not always happen naturally, they sometimes need to be created. When we do so we are vulnerable, because we have opened ourselves up to the possibility of rejection. This can be very painful. If we are not motivated by compassion, then we will give up sooner or later.

In Matthew 23:37 Jesus was looking over

Jerusalem, possibly with tears in his eyes when he said, *O Jerusalem, Jerusalem, you who kill the prophets and stone those sent to you, how often I have longed to gather your children together, as a hen gathers her chicks under her wings, but you were not willing*. This was a cry filled with deep compassion for people who were spiritually lost. Jesus so loved them, he so understood their plight, that he travelled the countryside preaching and urging them to turn to God. Undeterred by constant rejection, he went all the way to the cross, so that he could make salvation possible.

It is this compassion that we need if we are going to witness fearlessly for Christ. Only when we begin to care as Jesus cared, will we have the determination and resolve to overcome discouragement and share our faith, even in the face of a negative reaction.

This compassion is not something we can engineer. It is deeply rooted in our relationship with Christ. As we grow closer to him, so his values and thoughts become ours. We begin to feel his love and concern for others around us. This concern will grow into a sincere and selfless compassion that will endure and withstand the pressure of our worst mood and most cynical thought. This compassion will drive us to try and try again as we tell others of God's love for them.

At this point you may well be listing some excuses for not actively sharing your faith. Most Christians do! If there is something we really do not want to do, we are able to think of dozens of excuses as to why it is simply impossible to do it. Perhaps the most common excuse is, 'I am just not a good communicator'. We delude ourselves into thinking that we would be ineffective as evangelists, if we are not naturally charismatic personalities. The truth is that our fluency of conversation will do less than our sincerity. If you really believe something, then your earnestness will be evident however hard you might find it to talk to others about your faith.

Moses offered this excuse to God (Ex. 4:10), but clearly such an excuse is unacceptable. In Acts 1:8, Jesus promised that his followers would receive power from the Holy Spirit to help them in their witnessing. Prior to that he had promised that even under great pressure they would be able to present a defence of their faith. When we are concerned about our inability to communicate we need to remember these promises. The Holy Spirit will enable us to tell others about Christ. I have found, in many conversations with non-Christians, that relevant thoughts and ideas have readily come to mind which have helped me communicate my faith.

Whatever excuses we offer for not witnessing, they are simply not good enough. As followers of Christ one of our goals in life should be to encourage others to follow him also. However afraid we are, whatever the difficulties involved in witnessing for him, we should be prepared to pay the price of reaching others for him.

It is important that you begin witnessing now. Otherwise many opportunities will pass you by. It may be that you are looking for some specific steps which will enable you to start. Allow me to suggest a few ideas.

1. Think about two friends of yours who are not Christians. Pray for them by name once a week and ask God to give you opportunities both to show love to them and also to talk to them about your faith. Discover any objections they may have against Christianity and sensitively try and answer them. Use every opportunity to share your faith, but make sure you do it in a natural way. You also need to ensure that the way you live will not put them off becoming Christians.

2. Think about two people whom you know, but are not close enough to be called friends. Pray for them too and ask God to show you ways in which you could get to know them better. This may mean inviting them to your home or showing some other kindness. Make it your purpose to build such a relationship with them that you would not be embarrassed sharing your faith with them or perhaps inviting them to an event in your church.

3. Try to find ways of coming into contact with people who are not Christians. You may find that joining a sports club or some other society will help. Perhaps there are people who work for your company or school that you could get to know if

you made the effort. You might want to hold a house-party for the people in your street or be part of some social event in your area. However you do it, get to know people. Use whatever opportunity you have to live and talk about the Christian faith.

PRAYER:

Father, thank you for those people who first told me about your love. Thank you for the privilege of being an ambassador, representing your kingdom to the community in which I live.

Give me a compassion for people who do not know you. Give me a heart like Jesus, who wept for a dying world. Help me to share your love with my friends, work colleagues, and anyone who is prepared to listen.

Give me opportunities to witness for you and the courage to make the most of those opportunities. My desire is to lead other people to you so that you can save them also. Amen.

Chapter 13

The Guide

How do I know what God wants me to do with my life? This is the most logical question any Christian could ask. Hopefully you and I are interested in what God wants us to do with our lives. After all, a Christian is someone who has surrendered his life to God and allowed him to take control.

What then does God want me to do with my life? This leads us to the important subject of guidance. We know that God is interested in our lives. We also know that we will have to give an account for the lives we have lived (2 Cor. 5:9, 10). It is important, therefore, to spend our lives doing God's will.

Geography and Lifestyle

Before we look at how God guides, it is important to make some general statements about guidance. Firstly, I want to say that guidance has a little to do with geography and a lot to do with lifestyle. By that I mean how we live is the starting point, not where we live. It is true that God asks some Christians to go to a specific area and do a specific work. My father, for example, believed God was calling him to go to Ethiopia to be a missionary. This, however, is the exception rather than the rule.

It may well be that God asks you to go to a certain

country or area, but God definitely wants you to live a holy life. There is little point in seeking God's guidance if the life you are living displeases him. Whether you are living in Ethiopia, Hong Kong, Brazil or England, if your life does not match up to the Biblical requirements of Christian living, then you are not in God's will. Let me repeat again, the starting point for guidance is not where you should go, but how you should live.

The Spirit-Activated Mind

Secondly, when it comes to practical matters like what job should I go for, what house should I buy (or rent), what career should I choose or who should I marry, God expects me to use my own common sense. I am not saying that God does not want to be part of my decision making processes for I know he does. But I need to realise that God has given me a brain and he expects me to use it. As a Christian I want to please him and this attitude will therefore have an effect on how I make choices.

As God transforms me through his Holy Spirit, my very thought processes are being renewed. I am being made more like Jesus. It is therefore perfectly valid for me to use my mind and my ability to reason when I am searching for God's will. I can make perfectly valid choices in life based on my knowledge of God's character. It is also possible for other Christians to be of help in this area. Why not ask for advice from someone who knows you well and who is a mature Christian. They too can exercise their

Holy Spirit-activated mind in helping you discover what God is saying.

The Guide

Thirdly, we should not assume that guidance will always be elusive. It is true that sometimes I have had to wait for a long time before God has shown me what he wants me to do, but this again is the exception rather than the norm. God after all wants me to know his will. He is a loving Father who wishes the best for me and will therefore lead me clearly. To facilitate his guidance, God has given each of us his Holy Spirit. We are not just given some complex map of our lives and left to get on with it. The Holy Spirit lives in us and continually prompts us to follow God's will. In this sense we have a guide rather than just guidance.

A Correct View of God's Will

Fourthly, I do not believe that God's will for my life and yours follows a rigid pattern. Some Christians imagine that there is only one path they can follow, one job they can get, one partner they can marry or one house they can live in. If they do not find the right one then they are out of God's will. Personally I do not accept this view. Let us remember that God's will is more about lifestyle and less about geography. God is not an angry autocrat who looks down from the heavens waiting for me to make a mistake so that he can punish me. He is a loving Father who wants the best for me. He does have a plan for my life, but his plans are not about nit-picking, they are plans to fulfil and challenge me as a Christian, and plans that will make my life fruitful.

Having made the above statements I now want to answer the original question, how do I know what God wants me to do with my life? Or to rephrase the question how does God guide?

Willingness

The first comment that I would like to make is that God guides people who want to be guided. There is little point in seeking God's will if we are not going to be obedient to it. After all why should God reveal what he wants for us if we are just going to walk away from it? Our willingness to follow God's will and our desire to find out what it is can be expressed in prayer. For this reason prayer is the starting point of guidance.

As we pray we are acknowledging that we want what God wants. It is through prayer that we ask God to lead us and reveal what he wants us to do. Jesus stressed that if we ask we will receive (Matt. 7:7); with that in mind we should pray with a sense of confidence, believing that our prayer will be answered. He also said that if we seek we will find (Matt. 7:8). When we pray, therefore, we should also be looking for the different ways in which God guides. Alertness and sensitivity are important.

The Bible

Assuming that we are praying for guidance and seeking God's will, the next thing we need to consider is the Bible itself. God guides us through the Bible.

Let me qualify this by saying that we need to use the Bible properly when we look for guidance.

A young man was interested in a girl in his youth fellowship. The only problem was that they were both about to start university. He was going to Edinburgh and she to London. He began to look for God's guidance as to what to do about a relationship and as he opened his Bible he immediately saw Ruth 4:13, *So Boaz took Ruth and she became his wife*. As a result of this 'guidance' a relationship began.

This is not how the Bible should be used. It is not some lucky dip. I am not saying that this relationship was wrong, but you cannot take verses from the Bible at random and use them as justification for your actions. The Bible tells us how we should live our lives, it does not tell us the fine details of our daily actions.

I know of another situation where the Bible was used legitimately by someone who was seeking guidance. This situation also involved a relationship. The girl in this case was a Christian and her boyfriend was not. He wanted to marry her and she began to look for an answer in the Bible. She came across 2 Corinthians 6:14, *Do not be yoked together with unbelievers* and realised that entering into this marriage would involve disobeying a Biblical command. As a result of this guidance she broke off her relationship. This is a good example of how the Bible can be used when seeking God's will for our lives.

Circumstances

Another important element in guidance is circumstances. God is the Sovereign of the universe and everything is under his control. It is hardly surprising, therefore, that God uses circumstances to guide us. Jonah discovered this when he tried to run from God's will. He got on a ship heading in the opposite direction to where God wanted him and God sent a storm to halt the ship's progress (Jonah 1:4). Jonah could clearly read the circumstances and admitted to the crew, *I know that it is my fault that this great storm has come upon you* (Jonah 1:12).

I can remember a situation in my life where circumstances clearly guided me. I had been at Bible college for three years and was very interested in full-time Christian work. The only problem was I really didn't know where. I had prayed for several countries and would have been happy to go to any one of them, but what would I do when I got there?

After much thought I wrote to a friend of mine who ran a missionary training school in Scotland. I thought he could give me some advice. It so happened that a member of staff had left the training school and they were looking for a replacement. When I wrote I was completely unaware of this. Perhaps this could be called a coincidence. Someone looking for a job, writing unwittingly to someone else who is looking to fill a vacancy. For me it was guidance and the ensuing peace that I felt after I made the decision to go to Scotland has confirmed the rightness of the move.

God does use circumstances. Things do not just happen in our lives by accident. Our lives are not beyond God's control. For the Christian, coincidence is when God does something and decides to remain anonymous.

An Inner Voice

Another importance element in guidance is the inner voice. Jesus said, *My sheep listen to my voice; I know them, and they follow me* (John 10:27). This voice with which Jesus speaks is not audible, indeed it can only be heard by Christians. As we grow spiritually, we become increasingly aware of the spiritual world around us. Through prayer we talk to God and he talks to us, primarily through the Bible, but also through this inner voice.

You may want to call it a conscience. Perhaps even a gut feeling. But I have noticed as I have grown as a Christian, that God has spoken to me in this way. True this could be dismissed by the sceptic as just a subjective feeling. Never-the-less God speaks and those Christians who are mature and who know the voice of God will respond.

I talked earlier about the peace I felt when I came to Scotland. That was the inner voice. Up until that point I was so restless. With every option I considered my mind was in turmoil. Somehow I had this feeling that I had yet to discover what God really wanted. Subjective, perhaps, but very real to me. Equally real was the peace I felt when a job was offered to me in Scotland. I just knew this was what God wanted me to do.

Usually when God is guiding a person, all three of these avenues are used. You may find that your circumstances are leading you in a certain direction. You know from the Bible how you should respond in such a situation and you get an inner peace about the decision you are making. This is God's guidance. The important thing for you is to learn to be sensitive to his voice and to obey.

The Full Life
I have discovered over the last decade and a half that the Christian life is exciting, challenging and fulfilling. Note I did not say easy for it has never been that. Some of the toughest experiences I have ever gone through have happened since I became a Christian. I believe this is true of all Christians. But it has been more than worthwhile.

Jesus said, *I have come that they might have life and have it to the full* (John 10:10). Before I became a Christian I imagined that it must be a boring life. A life full of inhibitions and greatly lacking in zest. Clearly my experience has been otherwise. Not only do I live a life that is fulfilling, but this life will never end. One day, long after my body has rotted in the grave, the real me will live on in the paradise that Jesus talked about (John 14:2-3). There I will experience the glory of God in all its fullness, as I will also after the resurrection, as I share eternity with you and all our other brothers and sisters. Praise God!

What I look forward to on that day is to see Jesus

face to face. To look at the scars in his hands and to worship him for his great love. In 1 Corinthians 9 Paul talks about the Christian race. In Paul's day athletes were given a laurel wreath when they won a race (today's equivalent may be a medal). But those who run in the Christian race *do it to get a crown that will last forever* (v. 25). Whatever this crown is it has eternal value. There are rewards for Christians who run the race of the Christian life well. Paul longed for his reward (2 Tim. 4:8). So, I hope, do I.

You may have only just started in this race. It could be that you have only been a Christian for a few weeks or months. You are beginning to discover what is involved in your commitment to Jesus Christ. In this book I have tried to outline some of the first steps that you must take as a young Christian. This is only the beginning and you have your whole Christian life ahead of you.

Let me encourage you to keep going. Listen to God's voice as he speaks to you, guiding you in different ways. Be obedient no matter what the cost. Jesus will come again and establish his eternal kingdom and we as Christians will share eternity with him. This is your destiny, run the race of the Christian life, run it with all your might. Never give up or compromise. Do not lose heart. Keep in close contact with God and he will strengthen you for this exciting life that will never end. Live each day with your spiritual eyes firmly fixed on Jesus, your Shepherd, Saviour and Example.

PRAYER:

Father, thank you that you have a plan for my life, and that your plan is the best for me. Thank you that you take an interest in my life and that you are willing to show me what you expect of me.

Help me to be sensitive to your voice as you guide me from day to day. As I read your word and pray, as I interpret my circumstances and listen to the inner voice, speak to me and help me to obey. Help me to run the race of the Christian life with all my might. I pray that my life will glorify you. Amen.

Appendix

Bible Reading Programme

The Bible contains 1,189 chapters. In this Bible reading programme you will get an overall view of the Bible by reading just 245 chapters. Not every book of the Bible is in this list, for example I have not included 1&2 Chronicles, Esther, Job, Lamentations, Ezekiel, Obadiah, Micah, Nahum and Zephaniah from the Old Testament or Titus, Philemon, 2&3 John or Jude from the New Testament. But every section of the Bible is covered.

Try to read a couple of chapters each day and make notes about anything you have learned.

Old Testament

Genesis: The book of Genesis deals with important subjects such as the origin of man and the universe. As you read the opening chapters you will discover how sin came into the world, destroying the relationship between mankind and God. You will also real about God's love as he established a relationship with one man, Abram, and also with his descendants, the Jewish race (nation of Israel).

(25 chapters) 1-8, 15-16, 21-22, 27-28, 32, 37, 39-46, 50

Exodus: Exodus tells an exciting story of liberation. God calls Moses to lead the nation of Israel out of their captivity in Egypt and into the promised land. This book also contains the Ten Commandments, laws which God commanded his people to obey as part of their relationship with him.

(10 chapters) 1-3, 7, 11-12, 14, 19-20, 32

Leviticus: This book gives a detailed account of laws and regulations which the nation of Israel was expected to keep. Chapter 26 summarises the purpose of these laws.

(1 chapter) 26

Numbers: The book of Numbers is not only about the numbers of people in the nation of Israel, but we are also given a glimpse into their forty year journey through the desert before they entered the promised land. You will discover that despite all of God's goodness to them, the people were not always grateful.

(4 chapters) 1, 11, 14, 33

Deuteronomy: This book is a reiteration of the covenant (agreement) between God and his people, Israel. You will read about commands given by God, and also the handover of power from Moses to Joshua.

(5 chapters) 1, 6, 8, 31, 34

Joshua: This book deals with the exploits of Joshua (Moses' successor) as he leads the nation of Israel into the promised land.

(6 chapters) 1-2, 6-8, 24

Judges:Judges is a book about freedom fighters who defended Israel against her enemies. This book demonstrates that many of the people God used were flawed characters at best.

(6 chapters) 6-7, 13-16

Ruth: This 'romantic' book is about two women, a widow and her daughter-in-law, who find a man who is willing to take care of them amid difficult circumstances. Clearly they are under the watchful and loving eyes of God.

(4 chapters) 1-4

1 and 2 Samuel: These two historical books deal with the life and times of three leaders of Israel; Samuel, Saul and David. Though all had their faults, Samuel and David pleased God and led the people well. Saul on the other hand did more harm than good.

1 Samuel: (13 chapters) 1-3, 10, 15-20, 24, 26, 31

2 Samuel: (5 chapters) 1, 5-6, 11-12

1 and 2 Kings: These two books begin describing a 'Golden Age' under King Solomon (son of David). Things began to go wrong, however, as some of Solomon's foolish decisions caused rumblings of unrest. Eventually the kingdom of Israel is split in two with both the newly formed nations having a chequered history and finally being taken into exile by foreign powers.

1 Kings (5 chapters) 1, 3, 10, 17-18

2 Kings: (7 chapters) 1-2, 5, 17-20

Ezra: The books of Ezra and Nehemiah are a history of the repatriation of Jerusalem by the exiles. You will read about the rebuilding of the Temple and the walls of the city. Both men are an example of godliness and good leadership.

(5 chapters) 1, 3, 7, 9-10

Nehemiah: (6 chapters) 1-2, 4-6, 13

Psalms: The book of Psalms is loved by many, not only because of its poetry, but also because of the rich and varied emotions expressed. The Psalms were written by a number of people, most notably King David, and they express the true feelings of their authors during both good times and bad.

(9 chapters) 1, 18, 40, 42, 51, 62, 71, 92, 119

Proverbs: This is a book of sayings which encourage the reader to live a life characterised by wisdom and understanding.

(5 chapters) 4, 10, 15, 24, 31

Ecclesiastes: This fascinating and somewhat philosophical book debates the meaninglessness of life without God.

(3 chapters) 3, 5, 12

Songs: This book is full of love poems which describe the beauty of sexual love. Sexuality, after all, is a gift from God.

(2 chapters) 1, 4

Isaiah: Isaiah was a man who not only preached to the people of his day but also prophesied about some of the things God was going to do in the future. Some of these prophesies even deal with the life and death of the coming Messiah, Jesus Christ. This book deals with judgment and salvation.

(4 chapters) 6, 40, 53, 55

Jeremiah: Jeremiah too was a prophet as well as a realist. This book deals with some of his experiences and visions.

(5 chapters) 1-2, 15, 29, 38

Daniel: This is the story of a young boy who was taken into captivity, but learned to trust and obey God. As a result God used Daniel to convey visions to the people.

(4 chapters) 1, 3, 5, 6

Minor Prophets: This collection of books tell the story of men who were used by God to speak to their generation.

Hosea:	(4 chapters)	1-3, 14
Joel:	(1 chapter)	2
Amos:	(3 chapters)	4-5, 7
Jonah:	(4 chapters)	1-4
Habakkuk:	(1 chapter)	3
Haggai:	(1 chapter)	1
Zechariah:	(2 chapters)	7-8
Malachi:	(1 chapter)	3

New Testament

The Gospels: Tell the story of the life of Jesus Christ and his teaching.

Matthew:	(8 chapters)	1, 2, 5-7, 26-28
Mark:	(6 chapters)	1, 3, 6, 7, 9, 13
Luke:	(8 chapters)	1, 2, 10, 11, 15, 18, 24
John:	(11 chapters)	1-3, 6, 8-11,15, 17, 21

Acts: This is the story of the early church and the expansion of Christianity throughout the Roman empire. Two characters, Peter and Paul, are the particular focus of attention as they play their significant roles within the early church.

(12 chapters) 1, 2, 4, 6, 7, 9, 10, 13, 15, 17, 26, 28

Paul's Letters: This collection of the writings of Paul provides us with a great deal of important doctrinal and practical material. His letters were written to churches across the empire, encouraging them to continue in their new found faith.

Romans:	(6 chapters)	1, 3, 6, 12-14
1 Corinthians:	(6 chapters)	1, 5, 6, 12, 13, 15
2 Corinthians:	(5 chapters)	4, 5, 8, 9, 12
Galatians:	(3 chapters)	2, 3, 5
Ephesians:	(3 chapters)	2, 4, 6
Philippians:	(4 chapters)	1-4
Colossians:	(2 chapters)	1, 3
1 Thess:	(1 chapter)	4
2 Thess:	(1 chapter)	2
1 Timothy:	(4 chapters)	1-3, 6
2 Timothy:	(2 chapters)	2, 3

Hebrews: This book is written to Jewish Christians and shows how Jesus is the fulfilment of what was promised in the Old Testament.

(8 chapters) 1, 2, 5, 6, 9-12

James: This practical book teaches us some basic lessons of Christian living.

(5 chapters) 1-5

1 Peter: Practical teaching from Peter

(2 chapters) 1, 4

1 John: Practical teaching from John

(3 chapters) 1, 3, 5

Revelation: This book ends by looking forward to the end of time when all true Christians worship God in heaven, but begins with some powerful lessons for churches.

(4 chapters) 1-3, 22

Stephen McQuoid currently lectures at Tilsley College, which is part of the ministry of Gospel Literature Outreach, Motherwell. His area of expertise is evangelism and doctrine. During the summer months Stephen is involved in leading groups of young folk doing short-term pioneering evangelism throughout Europe.

Together with his wife Debbie, he is involved in a church planting work in Viewpark, Uddingston. Stephen travels widely teaching and preaching in churches throughout Britain, and also reporting on the work of Gospel Literature Outreach. His desire to see churches planted and grow in Christ stems from his upbringing in Ethiopia and the work of his missionary parents.

HAMILTON COLLEGE LIBRARY